STONE, SKIN, AND SILVER

A Translation of
The Dream of the Rood

Richard J. Kelly
&
Ciarán L. Quinn

LITHO PRESS
Midleton, Co Cork, Ireland

First Published 1999 by Litho Press Co.,
Midleton, Co Cork, Ireland

BRITISH LIBRARY CATALOGUING IN PUBLICATION DATA
Kelly, Richard J.
Stone, skin, and silver : a translation of The Dream of the Rood
1.Jesus Christ - Crucifixion - Poetry 2. Dream of the rood
I. Title II.Quinn, Ciaran L.
829.1

1 871121 40 X

Front Cover: *The Vercelli Book (fols. 104v–105r) & The Brussels Cross*
Back Cover: *The Ruthwell Cross & The Brussels Cross*

Layout and design: Richard J. Kelly & Stephen O'Connell

Printed by Litho Press Co., Midleton, Co Cork, Ireland

STONE, SKIN, AND SILVER
A Translation of the Dream of the Rood

For
Andrew & Joan Kelly
and
Lorcan & Bernadette Quinn
who have shared in all our work

Ic þæs wuldres treowes
oft nales æne   hæfde ingemynd
ær ic þæt wundor   onwrigen hæfde,
ymb þone beorhtan beam   swa ic on bocum fand,
wyrda gangum,   on gewritum cyðan
be ðam sigebeacne.

'Full oft I took thought   of the Tree of glory
Not once alone,   ere I learned the truth
Of the radiant Cross   as I read it in books,
In the fullness of time   so set forth in writing
The tale of that Standard.'

from *Elene* (ll. 1251-6)

Table of Contents

Foreword

The Dream of the Rood, a literary landmark from the earliest history of the English language, forms the focus and inspiration for this book. The Introduction follows the tradition and significance of the Cross from its origins in the pre-Christian era up to the period of the poem (*circa* tenth century). The first reference to this Old English Cross poem is the fourteen-line runic poetic text engraved on the stone-sculptured Ruthwell Cross (*circa* mid-eighth century). The iconographic art of this cross is systematically summarized. A comprehensive analysis of the poem then ensues, discussing manuscript context, stylistic features, and thematic design. The final extant reference to this poetic text is a two-line verse inscription on the early twelfth-century Brussels Cross, the description of which concludes the textual analysis. The Introduction ends with the Translator's Note where editorial policies are outlined.

A succeeding series of plates heralds then the title of the book, *Stone, Skin, and Silver*. The initial plates which are the four sides of the Ruthwell Cross include a fine photographic rendering of the runic writing on the original cross that is now in the parish church at Ruthwell in Dumfries, Scotland. The full manuscript facsimile of *The Dream of the Rood* (fols. 104v – 106r of the Vercelli Book) follows and subsequently a photographic plate of the Brussels Cross which is plated in silver and gilded with gold.

The book's hub is with the texts and translations: the Ruthwell runic poetic text, *The Dream of the Rood*, and the Brussels Cross verse inscription. Careful attention has been given to render these texts with accuracy from their original contexts; each of their Modern English translations aims to be interpretatively accurate.

A brief compilation of contemporary Latin and vernacular Cross hymns and poems goes on to complement the Anglo-Saxon texts. Not only is the broader religious context indicated but their shared tradition. *Vexilla Regis Prodeunt* and *Pange Lingua* by Fortunatus and *Victimae Paschali Laudes* by Wipo were sung in the liturgy of Lent and Holy Week in the Medieval Church. The Mugrón and Blathmac extracts from the Irish tradition are meditative pieces on the role of the Cross as protector and in the history of salvation; both themes are emphasized in *The Dream of the Rood*.

·The second series of plates invoke the wider scope and range of the Cross tradition throughout Europe in the early Middle Ages. Cross representations in the Lindisfarne Gospels and the Book of Kells, silver- and gold-plated processional and pectoral crosses, and the free-standing crosses of Ireland and Scotland give witness to the universality of Cross art and to a tradition shared with the Ruthwell Cross, *The Dream of the Rood*, and the Brussels Cross.

An outline of the history of the Anglo-Saxon period (*circa* AD 449–1100) and a brief description of the characteristic linguistic features of Old English at this stage of the book support and replenish the reader with chronological contexts and some general linguistic background. Tables and charts are formulated for quick and easy reference. This section concludes with a series of drawings depicting the various historical representations of the Cross tradition and a chart of the contents of the Vercelli Book.

The Select Bibliography and the Glossary (which combines the three poetic texts) draw the book to a close. The bibliographical information provides the opportunity for further reading and research. The Glossary affords the opportunity for a coordinated and more detailed insight into the Anglo-Saxon words in the texts.

Acknowledgements

Special thanks to the academic and administrative staff of Kobe University, Japan, for their indispensable help and support in the completion of this book. Thanks in particular is due to the following: Prof. Takao Hashimoto, Dean of the Faculty of Cross-cultural Studies, Prof. Tadamichi Magata, Dean of the Faculty of Letters, Prof. Taketoshi Furomoto, Prof. Yoshio Tsuda, Prof. Koji Watanabe, Prof. Keiji Notani, Prof. Kiyomitsu Yui, and Prof. Masayuki Kato.

Sincerest appreciation to Prof. Hideka Fukui (Chairperson) and Prof. Michiko Mori of Otemae Women's University, Nishinomiya, Japan, whose joint-work on another academic and research project provided the inspiration for this present publication. Special acknowledgement should also be made to Prof. Éamonn Ó Carragáin and Dr. Elisabeth Okasha of the National University of Ireland, University College Cork, Ireland, and to Prof. Eric G. Stanley, Emeritus Bosworth & Toller Professor of Anglo-Saxon Literature at the University of Oxford, who were responsible for introducing me to the world of Old English and fostering in me a deep love and appreciation of its literature, especially the Christian texts.

Acknowledgement with thanks to the Boards of Trustees at the following libraries and institutions for their gracious permission to reproduce the series of photographic plates used throughout the book: The British Library, London; The British Museum, London; Capitolo Metropolitano di S. Eusebio, Vercelli, Italy; Cathédrale des SS. Michel-et-Gudule, Brussels, Belgium; Dúchas, Dublin; Dumbarton Oaks Museum, Byzantine Collection, Washington D.C.; Dommuseum zu Salzburg, Austria; Museo Cividale, Cividale, Italy; The National Museum of Ireland, Dublin; Royal Commission on the Ancient and Historical Sites of Scotland, Edinburgh; Scala Museum, Florence, Italy; Trinity College, Dublin; The Dean & Chapter, Durham Cathedral, England; and University of Durham, England. Individual acknowledgements are cited at the end of each plate or series of plates to these libraries and institutions.

For their personal help and assistance deep-felt gratitude is extended to Dr. Michelle P. Browne, Keeper of the Western Manuscripts at the British Library, London; Don Mario Capellino, Director, Capitolo Metropolitano di S. Eusebio, Vercelli, Italy; Dr. Derek Craig, Research Assistant, Corpus of Anglo-Saxon Stone Sculpture, University of Durham, England; Mr. John Fitzgerald, Librarian, and Mrs. Helen Davis, Special Collections Librarian, at the Boole Library, National University of Ireland, University College Cork, Ireland; Mr. Barry Foley & Mr. Ralph Depping, Computer Bureau, National University of Ireland, University College Cork, Ireland; Dr. Reinhard Gratz, Dommuseum zu Salzburg, Austria; Rev. Kevin O'Neill, President, St. Patrick's College Carlow, Ireland; and Ms. Ann van Ypersele de Strihou, Curator, Cathédrale des SS. Michel-et-Gudule, Brussels, Belgium.

Prof. Colin Meir, emeritus of the University of McGill, Montreal, Canada, and the University of Ulster, Northern Ireland, who provided impetus, the title, and his gift of love of literature, is owed a deep-felt debt. His wisdom and experience has enhanced this book in so many ways – impossible to articulate sufficiently. To my co-editor, Mr. Ciarán L. Quinn, most heartfelt thanks, as the work is greatly enriched by his original and excellent contribution. Finally, thanks to Mr. Bill O'Callaghan and his professional staff (in particular, Mr. Steven O'Connell) at Litho Press, Cork, Ireland, for the wonderful job they have done in typesetting and producing this book. I am deeply indebted to all the above mentioned persons and institutions, and where these words were too short and inadequate to many others not mentioned who have so generously assisted in revealing 'The Way of the Cross'.

Richard J. Kelly
The Feast of the Annunciation
Kobe University, Japan
25 March 1999

List of Figures

List of FiguresTables

List of Plates

List of Abbreviations

AB	*Anglia Beiblatt*
Archiv	*Archiv für Studium der neueren Sprachen und Literaturen*
ASE	*Anglo-Saxon England*
ASPR	Anglo-Saxon Poetic Records
BC	Brussels Cross
BCI	Brussels Cross Inscription
B.L.	British Library
BM	*The Burlington Magazine*
B.M.	British Museum
Catal.	Catalogue
CCSL	*Corpus Christianorum,* Series Latina (Turnhout)
Ch/s.	Chapter/s
Col.	Column
Cott. Tiber.	Cotton Tiberius
Cott. Vitell.	Cotton Vitellius
ed/s.	editor/s
EEMF	*Early English Manuscripts in Facsimile*
EETS	*Early English Texts Society*
ELN	*English Language Notes*
ES	*Englische Studien*
esp.	especially
f./fol./fols.	folio/s
FACS	Facsimile/s
JEGP	*Journal of English and Germanic Philology*
MÆ	*Mediaevalia*
Med. Aev	Medium Aevum
MLN	*Modern Language Notes*
MLR	*Modern Language Review*
MP	*Modern Philology*

MS	*Medieval Studies*
MS/S	Manuscript/s
n/nn.	note/s
no/s	number/s
NM	*Neuphilologische Mitteilungen*
N & Q	*Notes and Queries*
Neophil	*Neophilologus*
os	Ordinary Series
p/pp.	page/s
PG	*Patrologiae Graeca,* Cursus Completus
PL	*Patrologiae Latina,* Cursus Completus
PMLA	*Publications of the Modern Language Association of America*
pl.	plate
r	recto
RC	Ruthwell Cross
repr.	reprinted
RES	*Review of English Studies*
rev.	revised
SPEC	*Speculum*
ss	Supplementary Series
trans.	translation/translator(s)
v	verso
VB	Vercelli Book
Vol/s.	Volume/s
vv.	verses

Grammatical Terms

acc.	accusative		**pers.**	person
adj.	adjective		**pl.**	plural
adjvl.	adjectival		**pass.**	passive
adv.	adverb		**pers.**	person
anom.	anomalous		**pl.**	plural
com. adj.	composite adjective		**poss.**	possessive
conj.	conjunction		**pp.**	past/present participle
cons.	consonant		**prep.**	preposition
dat.	dative		**pres.**	present
def. art.	definite article		**pret.**	preterite
dem.	demonstrative		**pret. pres.**	preterite present
dem. adj.	demonstrative adjective		**pron.**	pronoun
f.	feminine		**prop.**	proper
gen.	genitive		**part.**	participle
imp.	imperative		**rel. pron.**	relative pronoun
impers.	impersonal		**sg.**	singular
ind.	indicative		**sv.**	strong verb
infl.	inflected		**subj.**	subjunctive
inst.	instrumental		**sup.**	superlative
m.	masculine		**voc.**	vocative
n.	neuter		**w.**	word, with
neg.	negative		**wk.**	weak
nom.	nominative		**wv.**	weak verb
pass.	passive			

Introduction

The Cross and Crucifixion in Scripture and Historical Art

Crucifixion, the sentence feared, an excruciating death, to which slaves and non-Romans in the Ancient Roman Empire were subject for grave and heinous crimes, was Persian and Oriental in origin. Both from the Bible and other early accounts of crucifixion it cannot be assumed that Jesus Christ carried the full cross to His place of execution. Historically, the cross-beam was customarily carried to the stance of the upright beam. The bearer, the accused, had his arms bound by nails or ropes to the cross-beam. The wooden upright and cross-beam were joined and secured and their cruciform constituted. Both man and wood were vertically elevated, the feet fastened, and the miscreant held in shame for all below to see. Binding ropes would have supportively maintained the weight and the body in place where the pegging of nails were insufficient to do so.[1]

Scriptural descriptions of these public and punitive measures although differing from the attested accounts of early Roman writers present important historical parallels. From history, the condemned were usually stripped naked; for biblical equivalence, the soldiers had Christ's clothing gratuitously divided among themselves (Mt 27:35). Names and titles were written on placards and hung around the neck. In the Scriptures, Pilate, the Roman procurator of Judea who pronounced sentence on Christ, had in cynicism affixed over His head the label of 'King of the Jews'. It was written in three languages: (a) Aramaic, the Judaic vernacular, (b) Greek, the Roman lingua franca, and (c) Latin, the official language of Roman administration (Mt 27:37; Mk 15:26; Lk 23:38; Jn 19:19-22). Raised no more than a metre above the ground those crucified could have received sustenance, as, for example, Christ was proffered sponged vinegar on the end of a reed (Mt 27:48; Mk 15:36). Victims' deaths were more attributable to hunger and thirst as often the crucified survived and endured for several days the pain of the suffering that had been inflicted until their ultimate expiration. Christ, in contrast, is said to have died within hours, namely by the ninth (3pm) (Mt 27:45; Mk 15:33; Lk 23:44).

The Crucifixion is referred to only from within the New Testament. It is Jesus, in the synoptic Gospels, who exhorts a 'denial of self' (Mk 8:34) and one's own worldly concerns for those who should take up their own cross and follow Him (Mt 10:38; 16:24; Mk 8:34; Lk 9:23; 14:27). Paul preaches that by the sacrifice on the Cross Christ unites both Gentile and Jew (Eph 2:16). The Cross, its scandal to the Jewish world, is redemptive and does not require the Judaic cleansing of initiatory circumcision (Gal 5:11). The Cross solely is His claim to truth (Gal 6:14). Those who are false are the Cross's adversaries (Phil 3:18). Those crimes, the sins of mankind, are absolved by His suffering in volition and becoming Victim on the Cross (Col 2:14). Metaphorically, those in imitation, Christians, must renounce and master the sensuality of the flesh which is crucified (Gal 5:24); Paul, through the Cross of Christ, is crucified to the world and the world to him (Gal 6:14).

Dispersed communities, litanies of persecution, and the Church's emerging theological and liturgical developments mark the earliest history of Christianity. The Cross, the 'accursed tree', as early Christian adherents held, was a symbol of atonement yet designated a moribund signifier of sufferance and disgrace. The early Roman catacombs, souterrains nurturing tacitly a faith which is related to us now through art and artefacts, omit or avoid the expression of the Cross. Other symbols conveyed allegories for and analogies to the importance of Christ: (a) the fish, commonly depicted, signified the widely known anagram in Greek, *ichthus*, 'Jesus Christ, Son of God, Saviour', (b) the Lamb of God (*Agnus Dei*) was another early portrayal, and (c) the initial and final letters of the Greek alphabet, Alpha and Omega, signified conjunctively the beginning and end, Creation and the Second Coming, Death and Resurrection.[2]

In AD 312, Emperor Constantine was inspired by a heavenly vision of the sign of the Cross on the eve of battle, his victory over his imperial counterpart, Maxentius, at Milvian Bridge near north of Rome. Constantine was converted to Christianity subsequent to the vision, according to accounts by Lactantius (*circa* AD 317) and also Bishop Eusebius of Caesarea (d. AD 339/40) who asserts

---

[1] For an account of the historical Crucifixion, see McKenzie (1966; repr. 1975), pp. 161-2.

[2] Literature on early Christian and medieval art is vast. See Cabrol & Leclerc (1907-50), Beckwith (1961), Grabar (1968), and Talbot Rice (1963; repr. 1997). On iconography, see Lowden (1997), Schiller (1971), and Weitzmann (1978).

Constantine's personal intimation of the revelation to him on oath. Succeeding from the political imbroglio Constantine had the provinces of Italy and Africa annexed to his own demesne of Britain, Gaul, and Spain; Christians achieved a societal freedom of faith, and Christianity, its first Roman Emperor. Constantine ordered the *chi-rho* monogram, called the *labarum*, which constituted the two initial Greek letters of the name of Christ, X P ('XPIETOE', *Christos*), as an emblem to be applied and adopted by state and military standards and banners, and on the altars of churches.[3]

Through further conquest Constantine went on to merge the then antipodal realms of the Roman Empire, both East and West. On his initiative a basilica was built, the Church of the Holy Sepulchre, over the alleged Crucifixional site, Golgotha in Jerusalem. Cyril of Jerusalem who preached to this church's congregation records *circa* AD 350 the discovery of a great Cross *in situ*. Pieces of the Cross were disseminated and a portentuous cruciform apparition of light was seen in the sky overhead. By the end of the fourth century a tradition, the Invention of the True Cross, became more widespread; the discovery of the True Cross was ascribed to Helena, Constantine's mother, and the occasion to her visit to the Holy Land in AD 326.[4] The Cross was soon of itself to become venerated.

According to the legend of Helena, the Gospel triad of crosses, the superscription whose words spurned Christ and the iron nails with which He was crucified were exhumed. A curative miracle established this to be the True Cross. Helena had a pair of its nails dispatched to Constantine, one enshrined in a crown, the other in a bridle; the other pair was said to have been forged to make a sword, or alternatively, a spear for the Emperor. The titled inscription came to be preserved at the Basilica of St. Croce, within Helena's own palace in Rome. A dispersal of fragments, relics of the True Cross, ensued and continued for many centuries afterwards throughout Christendom.

Two feasts of the Cross were commemorated by the Christian Churches within the liturgy, their services of public worship: (a) the ancient and major Eastern festivity of the Exaltation of the Holy Cross on 14 September, and (b) the feast of the Invention of the Holy Cross on 3 May within the liturgical calendar in the Western Church by the seventh century.

Within the Eastern Church theological debates about the nature of the visual image of God were deeply underscored by dissonance and discord.[5] In AD 726 an edict against deistic images, encouraged by Emperor Leo III, led to the destruction of the icon of Christ at the palace gate of Constantinople and the subsequent resignation of the Church Patriarch, Germanus, an advocate of images. Leo's son and heir, Constantine V, sided in solidarity with the Monophysites who believed that Christ embodied a single divine nature (or *physis*) indivisible from the incarnate Logos. The aniconic Cross alone remained apparently unscathed by controversy or censure.

In AD 787 the Second Council of Nicaea under the auspices of the widowed regent, Irene, and the Patriarch, Tarasius, iconoclasm was rescinded. The christological debate intensified when iconoclasm erupted once more in AD 813 under Emperor Leo V, who wished to emulate his earlier predecessors until an orthodoxy, the identity and nature of Christ as both human and divine, was restored in AD 843.

The Western Church did not standardize the visual image of God, provide visual uniformity or clearly defined functions based on theological precepts as which had occurred by the end of the iconoclastic period in Byzantium. The image could be non-mimetic, highly particularized due to either the detail of style or its context. Gregory the Great maintained the picture was informative of the uneducated. Although originally a concerted sixth-century missionary strategy, by the eighth Gregory's statements had come to authorize the instruction of the illiterate or uneducated.[6]

In early Anglo-Saxon England references to religious debate about the nature of the deistic image are few. Theodore of Tarsus, an Eastern theologian, presided over a pan-national assembly at Hatfield

---

[3] For an account of this historical period, see Collins (1991), pp. 16-30. On Constantine, see MacMullen (1984); on Eusebius, *PG*: XX. 944-5, 948; and on Lactantius, *PL*: VII. 260-2.

[4] On the construction of the basilica, see Eusebius in *PG*: XX. 1085; on the apparition at Golgotha, see *PG*: XXXIII. 468-9, 776-7, & 1168-9; on the 'Invention' tradition, see Ambrose in *PL*: XVI. 1463, and Rufinus in *PL*: XXI. 475-7.

[5] Literature on the image debate is vast. For a comprehensive historical summary, see Belting (1994), pp. 115-83, Kitzinger (1954), pp. 83-150; (repr. 1976), pp. 90-156.

[6] Gregory the Great, *Epistolae* IX. 209, & XI. 10 in *CCSL*: 140 & 140A. See also Kessler (1985), pp. 75-91.

(AD 679) at which the decrees of the Latern Council (AD 694) were adopted; these maintained that at the essence of His dual natures, human and divine, were two wills within the person of Christ.[7] In Northumbria Bede's Lives of the Abbots records Abbot Benedict Biscop's bringing from Rome (AD 680) images of the Virgin Mary, the twelve apostles, and Gospel and Apocalyptic scenes, for his church of St. Peter's at Monkwearmouth. From a subsequent and similar journey Biscop brought images for the church of St. Mary's at Monkwearmouth; these are believed to have been painted panels. The images at St. Peter's formed narrative cycles for the walls and inert portrayals for the area of sanctuary, most likely the chancel to the east of the nave which was segregated for the officiating clergy. The images could have been icons. An icon is a panelled portable image, its figuration solitary, static, and venerated. Bede, in commentary, assigns a pedagogical and spiritual role to pictures reminiscent of Gregory's assertions, which would have allayed such developments in worship.[8]

As we see them today the sculpted images on crosses are autonomous media of spiritual experience. They may not merely narrate episodes from the Life of Christ and His Passion but can transcend to inform and present spiritual significance or even engage empathy in the believer. In Western religious art of the early Middle Ages this freedom from textual scripture is manifest and manifold. The text of the Scriptures required elucidation within the Church, i.e. an exegesis that guided its interpretation. Two main divergent schools of exegesis existed which may have influenced art through their teachings: (a) the Alexandrine school which emphasized allegorical interpretation, and (b) the Antiochan school which stressed the historical and literal sense of Scripture.

Exegetical commentators maintained the symbolic significance of scriptural text on three to four levels. First was a literal sense that was most often closely aligned to the historical narrative of the Bible. This was conjoined with three further spiritual senses: allegorical, moral, and anagogical.[9] Each level acts as an addition of statement symbolically to the original text's significance. Augustine of Hippo (AD 354-430) rather than simply discuss or investigate meaning for Scripture also concentrates on the methodology of interpretation. He proposes that every figurative expression in the Bible was to be interpreted; the polyvalence of potential meanings allows for a proliferation of interpreters interpreting but all must affirm truth, the unity of meaning of the Bible. Gregory the Great writing about interpretation draws the analogy between a meandering river on how the commentator should readily digress.[10] Although all Christian interpretation of the Bible was infused with the selfsame message of redemptive salvation it was the modes and methods by which this was to be achieved that enthused both art and literature. Augustine proposed a search and confirmation of biblical truth, i.e. typology, which was Messianic and which stated that the New Testament is hidden in the Old while the Old is made clear by the New. In typology, Jonah and the Whale was symbolic of Christ's Resurrection, the Ark and Deluge symbolized or prefigured the waters of Baptism and Redemption. Although none of these Old Testament prefigurements has been said to occur on the Ruthwell Cross the foreshadowing of events and examplars as in the case of the depictions of the Annunciation or Mary Anoints the Feet of Jesus are evident.

A written text is linear; depiction concludes spatial relationships.[11] For interpretation both maintain latent meaning but both are read differently. Exegesis being in essence a textual analysis of the Scriptures and the sculptured art forms a religious commentary in its own right, a visual exegesis. Cross iconography cannot represent a direct visual exegetical equivalent of biblical text as it is abbreviated to a few panels on a cross; the term visual exegesis does not refer directly to biblical interpretation. It can otherwise portray religious motifs, signs, sequences, and narratives. It can conflate several ideas simultaneously. Detail, selection, arrangement, association, and sequence of the iconography are a central part of our analysis of the depictive commentary on the Cross.

---

[7] See Haddan & Stubbs (1871), III, pp. 145-51.

[8] On the history of the abbots, see Plummer (1896). On Bede's commentary on art, see *De Templo*, 2, & Homily, 1. 13 in *CCSL*: 119A & 122.

[9] On medieval exegesis, see de Lubac (1959-64), Simonetti (1994), Kannengiesser & Bright (1996).

[10] Gregory the Great, *Moralia sive Expositio in Job, Epistula Praevia ad Leandrum Hispalensem* in *PL*: LXXV. 513.

[11] A comprehensive account on the relationship between text and image is found in Barasch (1992), pp. 75 & 81. See also Raw (1997), p. 4. On modern trends on the theory of their inter-relation, see Mitchell (1987).

Free-standing crosses implied considerable investment both in skill and finances. What could be the purpose of these silent sentinels? The functions of stone crosses can be categorized into two broad divisions: (a) the Cross is a focus of authority and reverence instituting functions legal, contractual, and commercial, of sanctuary or of patronage; the iconography does not require essential viewing, (b) the interpretation of the art is integral to or the basis for the Cross's functions. The Ruthwell Cross could encompass both precepts. The art on the Ruthwell Cross is sophisticated, arrests visual immediacy, requires further thought. Audiences would, therefore, have been relatively educated, yet an exacting appraisal of their literacy skills would prove difficult; rote memorization, reading and recitation, writing and copying were learned abilities better defined and distinguishable than in the Modern Age.[12]

It is generally acknowledged that Northumbria engendered the seminal reality of the free-standing stone cross, preceded by wooden archetypes. The wooden cross is attested to only historically. Bede describes in his *Ecclesiastical History of the English People* (AD 731) King Oswald's having a wooden cross erected on the eve of battle against the Brittonic King Cædwalla at Heavenfield near Hexham (AD 634) as a standard for victory through faith and a focus for devotion.[13] Bede's account dubiously attributes its edifice as Bernicia's first Christian monument. According to his account, the wooden cruciform was still standing during Bede's lifetime when slivers of wood and the moss that had grown upon it were retained as curative and miraculous relics.

Non-Christian free-standing pillars and monoliths stood within countries, cultures, and communities with which converting Christianity complied, compromised, or defied. Bede makes reference to pagan idols of the seventh century, to Gregory the Great's advice to Augustine of Canterbury for their destruction yet the preservation of the physical sanctity of their erstwhile temples and restoration as churches. Apostasy was abhorred, the constancy of belief was in its fragility a vitreous observance. In AD 664 the Synod of Whitby caused controversy.[14] A new dating and computus for Easter, an ordinance from Rome, was adopted by the Anglo-Saxon Northumbrian Church which directly caused the dissipation of alliances, political, and ecclesiastical, with dissenting Celtic Irish factions. In its wake, the outbreak of an epidemic precipitated a recalcitrant regression for Christians to the worship of pagan idols in nearby Bernicia and in Essex. Yet even Christian symbols could be subject to discrediting disparagement; in AD 744, Boniface castigated how erected crosses were distracting from regular church services.

King Oswald who was converted at Iona in western Scotland may have been influenced by Cross developments at this central Celtic Christian monastic site. Adomnán (d. AD 704), the ninth abbot of Iona, refers in his hagiographical *Life of St. Columba* to the siting of three commemorative crosses.[15] These were presumably wooden and although their chronology is unclear they well antedate the eighth-century establishment of the decorated stone crosses of SS. John, Oran, and Martin on the island of Iona.

Arculf's seventh-century Latin account of the Orient and Holy Land, *De Locis Sanctis* ('Of Holy Places'), describes Cross relics at Byzantium, a commemorative silver cross at Golgotha which replaced a fifth-century jewelled cross plundered by the Persians in AD 614, and one of wood held at stance in the Jordan where Christ was baptized. Adomnán had its translation dedicated to the Northumbrian Aldfrith (AD 685-704) to be copied and distributed.[16] The impact and impetus of such accounts, the role and influence of the imputed tactile witnesses to Christ's Passion, fragments of the True Cross, although intellectually definable their spiritual significance is unquantifiable.

---

[12] On Anglo-Saxon pedagogy, refer to Riché (1976), Sims-Williams (1990), pp. 177-210, and Lendinara (1991).

[13] See Bede's *Ecclesiastical History of the English People*, Bk. III, Ch. II in Colgrave & Mynors (1969; repr. 1992).

[14] On the Church Synod of Whitby, refer to Bede's *Ecclesiastical History of the English People*, Bk. III, Ch. XXV-XXVII in Colgrave & Mynors (1969; repr. 1992).

[15] See *The Life of St. Columba*, Bk. I. 45 in Anderson, & Anderson (1961; repr. 1991).

[16] See Adomnán's translation in Meehan (1958).

The Ruthwell Cross

The extant *oeuvre* of an unknown monastic community in west Northumbria, the Ruthwell Cross, now stands some 5m 28cm in height by the baptistery in a small church on the outskirts of the village of Ruthwell, due south of Dumfries in Scotland. The cross, perceived as an irreverent idolatry, was torn down and dismembered in 1642 by order of the General Assembly of the Church of Scotland. In 1887 Henry Duncan, the Ruthwell church minister, had its fragments of local red sandstone, which had lain neglected in the churchyard, reassembled and the cross reconstructed from where it was later placed in its present position. Unfortunately, the transom (or cross-beam) was not recovered and was imaginatively refashioned. The present depictive abstract and animal menagerie is ill-conceived yet consummates the three-dimensional contour of the cross.[17]

The securing of an accurate date for the establishment of the cross has caused considerable debate. Discussions have not reached comprehensive conclusions. The arguments that have been explored are (a) stylistic, (b) epigraphical and philological, and (c) historical.[18]

Stylistic arguments are essentially founded on comparative patterns, tracery, and motifs, and where accompanying epigraphical evidence is applicable. Collingwood determined that adept carving in stone in the north of England could not have been perpetuated until the decoration of churches was established.[19] The double-stranded interlace flanking the sides of the related Bewcastle Shaft he attributed a date and for the Ruthwell Cross to *circa* AD 750. Vine-scroll ornamentation indicates Eucharistic significance but ultimately antecedes from classical and Mediterranean tradition. Baldwin Brown held Anglo-Saxon models as generically Grecian rather than Roman;[20] Kitzinger formulated Eastern models for the late eighth century, but surmises possibilities of unknown occidental modes of transmission from Late Antiquity.[21] R. Cramp has proposed textiles, evidence for whose importation is in abundance, as probable modes of stylistic transmission. She has contended differing dates for both Ruthwell and Bewcastle vine-scroll ornamentation: (a) in 1960-5 she determined their chronology in accordance with two inhabited (i.e. those containing birds and quadrupeds which in depiction partake of the vine) vine-scroll stone fragments at Jarrow *circa* AD 750, whose provenance is not conclusively Jarrow, and (b) more recently, she has forwarded earlier dates *circa* AD 700-50, although conceding inadequacies in the Jarrow parallelism.[22]

For the runic inscriptions R. I. Page originally proposed dates from between AD 750 to AD 850 for both the Ruthwell and the proximate Bewcastle Shaft, subsequently retracting the chronological span from AD 650 to AD 750. For the Bewcastle Shaft he also cautions that corruption caused by nineteenth century runic enthusiasts' carvings complicates a melange amongst its original 'unusual and linguistic forms.'[23] Higgit posits the Latin inscriptions as later than the dedicatory Jarrow inscription (*circa* AD 685) and the Cuthbert's coffin incision (*circa* AD 698) while being in precedence of the early ninth-century flourishment of the manuscript scripts of the Lichfield Gospels and the Book of Kells.[24]

From historical sources, MacLean concludes that such early dates as AD 685 are untenable for the Ruthwell Cross. These sources relied upon are Anglo-Saxon, more specifically Bede, who does not clarify which lands were settled by Northumbrian conquests throughout the region and the seventh century. Baldwin Brown and Schapiro do not acknowledge the significance of the embattled Celtic Briton kingdom of Rheged as being disparate from the Briton kingdom of Strathclyde which was centred at Dumbarton to the north;[25] Rheged was centred at Carlisle and contained the community at

---

[17] Meyvaert (1982), pp. 4-5, and Meyvaert (1992) in Cassidy (1992), pp. 95-104.

[18] On a comprehensive study on the chronological dating of the Ruthwell Cross, see MacLean in Cassidy (1992), pp. 49-70.

[19] Collingwood (1918), pp. 34-83.

[20] Brown (1921), pp. 102-317.

[21] Kitzinger (1936), pp. 61-71.

[22] Cramp (1959-60), pp. 12-3, Cramp (1965), pp. 8-12, Cramp (1984), pp. 27, 114-5, Bailey & Cramp (1988), pp. 20-1, 71.

[23] Page (1959b), pp. 50-3. See also Page (1973), p. 148.

[24] On Higgitt's comment, see MacLean in Cassidy (1992), p. 54, n. 24.

[25] Brown (1921), pp. 291-5, and Schapiro (1944), p. 241.

Ruthwell some twenty miles due east. It is not clear that Carlisle was territorily Northumbrian until the death of King Ecgfrith, at the hands of the Picts at the Battle of Dunnichen (named Nechtanesmere by Simeon of Durham) in AD 685. These recent Northumbrian acquisitions of Rheged could not have been consolidated nor the erection of free-standing monuments facilitated readily within the Ruthwell region till some years later.

The legacy of Rheged is preserved in the earliest extant Welsh literature. Prince Urien of Rheged, Lord of Catraeth (Catterick in Yorkshire to the east) is celebrated in poems attributed to Taliesin, of the late sixth century. The final demise and dissolution of Rheged, however, remains taciturn, lacking the epic elegy and eulogy of the Gododdin and their annihilation at Catterick (*circa* AD 600) which was immortalized in separate Welsh tradition by the battle's reputed sole survivor, the poet Aneirin.[26]

In summary, MacLean concedes a date from between AD 731 to AD 750 for the cross's erection.[27] Bede in his *Historia Ecclesiastica* (AD 731) makes reference to recent increases in the numbers of the faithful more westerly at Whithorn (*Candida Casa*), which necessitated the new establishment of a bishopric at this older Celtic sanctum of St. Ninian; this confirms the securing of vibrant Anglo-Saxon ecclesiastical structures beyond Ruthwell. The expansionist conquest by King Eadberht into the littoral Kyle region of Strathclyde in AD 750 belies an assuredness that Rheged to the rear and south was secure.

How and where was the Ruthwell Cross originally situated? Ó Carragáin maintains the cross as an outdoor focus of liturgical and spiritual monastic contemplation. For the opposite faces of the cross he formulates apposite liturgical significances, emblematic of baptism and the Eucharist.[28] Meyvaert proposes the cross's original intended placement within a church although no structure of such capacity has been ascertained. He argues as inverse the expression of the opposing iconographic faces: the East (now South) face stresses the Church (*ecclesia*) and the West (now North) face emphasizes monasticism (*monastica*).[29]

The Ruthwell Cross today should be regarded as isolated but within a continuum; its full Northumbrian contemporary landscape was possibly invested with in excess of four hundred free-standing monuments. Cross-slabs, illuminated manuscripts, the array of metalwork, carvings and paintings in wood now lost, the etching in ivory, bone and stone could all have formed similitudes, prototypes, and models, and even the frozen features of the skeuomorph (i.e. an expression whose generic meaning had become unknown), for the transmission of style and detail.

The free-standing cross is almost invariably insular in tradition and is found widely throughout the British Isles. This tradition amalgamates connections and developments that are generically continental, innovations and considerations domestic. Since the Anglo-Saxon polity for the period is marked by jostling kingdoms and alliances so its expression in art is for analogy in part characterized: 'The insular tradition is not monolithic, there are perceptible regional and cultural differences, particularly between those who did and those who did not accept without adaptation Mediterranean traditions. This is a period of swift assimilation, which produces an art which is pattern-making and motif-making, breaking the flowing repetitive rhythms of classical art into isolated densely packed elements, and this remains an important aspect of Anglo-Saxon art right up to the Conquest.'[30]

Artefacts and authors were portable purveyors, mobile and constantly capable of change; this complicates our analysis and awareness of their provenance. Yet, the mutability of the manuscript and even of metalwork juxtaposes sharply with the inertia of the stone of the cross. The artistry of all artists is, however, contained by that 'in the transmission of pictorial models corruption may occur as the original intent and effect are garbled as a result of deficiency in the copyist's skill, a misunderstanding of the image in the model, the copyist's interpretation of the model according to the style in which he has been trained, or the artist's desire to improve upon the image, for instance, to

---

[26] For a summary, see MacLean in Cassidy (1992), pp. 61-8. On Urien of Rheged, see Dillon & Chadwick (1967), pp. 270-3. On the Gododdin, see Jackson (1969).

[27] See MacLean in Cassidy (1992), pp. 69-70.

[28] Ó Carragáin (1987), pp. 121-2. See also Meyvaert in Cassidy (1992), p. 108, n. 40.

[29] See Meyvaert in Cassidy (1992), esp. pp. 102-4.

[30] Cramp in Karkov, Ryan, & Farrell (1997), p. 295.

make it more suitable to a new context or to make it more contemporary.'[31] The stone sculpture of the Ruthwell Cross is to be dually appraised: the sculpture reveals the intellect to us that guides the choice and arrangement of religious themes and the skill and learning with which the sculptor has presented his subject.

Physicalities confound perception. The runic inscriptions 'are maddeningly hard to read.'[32] The Latin inscriptions that span the lateral divisions of the iconographic panels are highly condensed and contracted. The sheer towering stature of the monolith would hinder clear decipherment except at very close quarters. Rote memorization, a fundamental monastic instructional process, could have stimulated recall on recognition, even *in situ* recitation. However, mnemonics are not signified, the Latin inscriptions appear as if frozen in mid-sentence and the Ruthwell runic poetic text corresponds with a particular central rather than initiatory section of the later *Dream of the Rood* poem. It has been debated as whether these inscriptions were a later addition to the cross.[33]

A Summary of the Iconographic Programme

The iconographic panels are catalogued in numerical order from the bottom moving vertically upwards. To facilitate visual reference the original and present reconstructed form of the cross as it now stands in the church at Ruthwell has been adopted. The present reconstruction of the original fragments is apparently incorrect. Two readjustments to the upper panels can be proposed: (I) the face order of the top fragment above the transom, the Eagle (West (now North) face, Panel 7) and of John and the Eagle (East (now South) face, Panel 7), are to be reversed; (II) in conjunction with this reversal Meyvaert also proposes the inversion of Martha and Mary (East (now South) face, Panel 5) and the Archer (East (now South) face, Panel 6) with their opposite facing *Agnus Dei* (West (now North) face, Panel 5) and Matthew and the Man (West (now North) face, Panel 6).[34] The modern interpretations given are not definitive; their synopsis intends only an abbreviated commentary of the current focus in argument about the iconographic art.

East (now South) Face

Panel One: The Crucifixion Scene

The cruciate Christ was offered cheap wine on a reed (Mt 27:48; Mk 15:36; Lk 23:36) or 'vinegar about hyssop' (Jn 19:29); on realizing Christ is already dead a soldier pierces His side with a lance (Jn 19:34, 37). In the apocryphal Gospel of Nicodemus, the soldiers are singularly named: Stephaton, who offered vinegar to Christ on the Cross, and Longinus who pierced His side with the lance. They are illustrated acting simultaneously in Crucifixion scenes, flanking to the right and left respectively; Christ is both alive and dead, expressing His humanity and divinity in hypostatic union. The Ruthwell Cross portrays, as was common, a concomitant *sol* and *luna*, the sun and crescent moon, on opposite and upper sides of the transom. 25 March represented the liturgical significance for Good Friday that was a moveable feast. They are also significant of the scriptural account of how the earth darkened from the sixth till the ninth hour when Christ's life on earth ended (Mt 27:45; Mk 15:33; Lk 23:44).[35]

Panel Two: The Annunciation

The Annunciation (Lk 1:28) depiction panel is notably and directly above the Crucifixion scene. The conception of Christ, celebrated in the liturgy on 25 March, was symbolically synonymous with the date of the Crucifixion, twelve months later. The Annunciation, heralding Christ's conception, was forwarded by Bede as 'the beginning of our redemption' and 'the restoration of mankind', a clear Crucifixion theme.[36]

---

[31] Netzer (1994), p. 56.
[32] Page (1973), p. 150.
[33] Stanley (1987).
[34] See Meyvaert in Cassidy (1992), p. 104.
[35] See Meyvaert in Cassidy (1992), pp. 106-8. On the Crucifixion in Anglo-Saxon Art, see Raw (1990). An edition of the Apocryphal Gospel of Nicodemus is in James (1953).
[36] See Meyvaert in Cassidy (1992), pp. 108-9. Bede's homily for Advent is in *CCSL*: 122, 14, 11, 1, 10.

Panel Three: The Healing of the Man Born Blind

In patristic commentary the blind man was seen as allegorically symbolic of humanity; enlightenment was to be achieved through his healing. The scene was well represented in early medieval art. This was widely used as a Gospel lection reading (Jn 9:1-38) throughout the Western Church on the Fourth Week in Lent. From the early Christian Church this liturgical week celebrated the third and most important of the seven exorcizing scrutinies of the catechumens in their preparation for baptism at the Easter Vigil. It also celebrated the symbolical handing on (*Traditio Evangeliorum*) of the *Credo* and *Pater Noster* to those to be newly initiated into the faith.[37]

Panel Four: Mary Anoints the Feet of Jesus

The inscription which surrounds this depiction refers directly to Lk 7:37-38; in this scriptural narrative the identity of the penitent woman is unknown. In Mt 26:6-13 and Mk 14:3-9 an unnamed repentant woman anoints the head of Christ. Jerome in his commentary on Matthew distinguishes the woman of the Lucian narrative from the other two synoptic accounts. Bede rejecting this analysis identifies all women as the same and as being Mary Magdalene who is named in the Johnnine account (Jn 12:1-8).[38]

Panel Five: Martha & Mary/Visitation

This depiction reverberates with the relevance of debates concerning the identity of Mary Magdalene on the preceding panel. The epigraphical engraving which environs is in Latin but to exception carved in runic ciphers; the word Martha is from parts legible. Martha and Mary, worthy women, are referred to in Scripture as sisters in contraposition (Lk 10:38-42).[39] In exegesis Gregory the Great (later elaborated upon by Bede) envisages Martha as expressive of an *actualis vita*, an active life given spiritually to the extrinsic expression of administering to our neighbour; Mary voices *contemplativa vita*, an inner yearning for the love of our Lord. Seventh-century Isidore of Seville identifies Martha with the church of the world in the present and Mary, since contemplation is never fully realizable, with the church of the world to come.[40] Most recent scholarship on this panel interprets a Visitation scene indicating by close scrutiny that both figures place a hand on each other's womb.[41] Ó Carragáin (1999) states that only in the Roman liturgy of the late seventh and early eighth centuries was the story of the Visitation read at mass on the feast of the Nativity of the Virgin (September 8). Later in the eighth century this Visitation lection was replaced by the mass lection, the genealogy of Christ (Mt 1:17). The most significant of the new Marian feasts, introduced into the liturgy at this period, was the Assumption of the Virgin on 15 August.[42] The Gospel lection for this feast was the story of Martha and Mary from Luke's Gospel.[43]

Panel Six: The Archer

Readadjustment (I) places the eagle directly above the ring centre and archer. On an ivory pectoral cross, and the cross shafts of St. Andrew Auckland and Bradbourne an archer aims directly at the eagle. On the Ruthwell Cross, however, the archer aims at a roughly forty-five degree angle at the right transom arm. On the Scottish Camuston Cross a centaur braces and aims within the same panel position and at the same angle. On the Rothbury Cross shaft an archer is entangled in a vine-scroll at its base.

---

[37] See Meyvaert in Cassidy (1992), 109-10. On the *Traditio Evangeliorum*, see Ó Carragáin in O'Mahony (1994), pp. 398-436.

[38] See Meyvaert in Cassidy (1992), pp. 110-2. The Jerome text is in *PL*: XXVI. 199A, and the relevant Bede commentary on the Gospel of St. Luke is in *CCSL*: 120, pp. 166-7.

[39] Howlett (1974b), p. 334, offers this interpretation of the inscription.

[40] Following Gregory, see Bede's commentary on the Gospel of St. Mark in *CCSL*: 120, p. 225, and on Isidore of Seville, see *PL*: LXXXIII. 124D-125A.

[41] Sincere gratitude to Prof. Éamonn Ó Carragáin for pointing out his recent scholarship on this panel; refer to Ó Carragáin (1999).

[42] Ó Carragáin (1994), pp. 34-6.

[43] See Ó Carragáin (1999), pp. 3-4.

Scriptural references to archers, arrows, and bows are vast; their interpretations in consequence broader. Both Saxl and Schapiro make allusions to Ps 90(91):5 ('the arrow that flies by day') for the archer; while Farrell thoroughly explores this psalm's implications concluding a malign force as its likely symbolic import.[44]

Alternatively, the arrow could be perceived benign and beneficial, as conducive to the Cross of Victory. Augustine in his commentary on Ps 119:4 ('the sharp arrows of the powerful one') combines the image of hearts healed by the momentary transfixion by arrows, the words of God, and the convalescent living out of them through faith. Adding to Augustine's exposition of the sharp emphatic arrows of Ps 44:6, Cassiodorus maintains the wood of the arrow as the word of God emanating from the wood of the Cross.[45]

Panel Seven: St. John and the Eagle

With readjustment (I) this panel would be placed on the opposite face above (West (now North) face, Panel 6) Matthew and the Man. It may symbolize St. John and the Eagle. Its aquiline significance is evidentially linked to its counterpart, the Eagle, on the opposite side. The revelation of the Second Coming to which both eagle and John pertain may prove pertinent.

West (now North) Face

Panel One: Eroded and Unrecognizable

This panel has been interpreted as originally representing an early Nativity scene. This would be seen as associative and directly paralleling the Crucifixion scene on the opposite side. Interpretations arc, however, speculative.

Panel Two: The Flight Into/Out of Egypt

Henderson maintains this panel as the Return from Egypt arguing on the basis that the image, its narrative and action, adheres with conventional Western narrative direction, i.e. from left to right. Representations of the Holy Family and their journeys in and out of the desert are few. Early Irish and Northumbrian martyrologies refer to the importance of a liturgical feast, *Eductio Christi de Egypto*, which celebrates the Return. In the Irish vernacular *Martyrology of Oengus* (*circa* AD 800) a marginal note for this feast equates the word *Egyptus* (Egypt) with the word *tenebrae* ('darkness') and this coming out and return with joy.[46]

Panel Three: Paul and Antony

The representation of Paul and Antony reiterates and emphasizes the theme of the desert, recalling the forty years of Moses and the Israelites' wandering in the wilderness and the forty days of the Lenten fast. Monasticism was diametrically divided between a cenobitic (communal) and eremitic spirituality. Each sought the desert as a metaphorical exemplar for segregation from the contemporary world and secular society. The meeting of Paul the hermit with Antony in the desert based on Jerome's version of *Vita Pauli* epitomizes their monastic concurrence with an implicit symbolic Eucharistic significance. The narrative relates how Paul in the desert while awaiting the raven which for sixty years swooped down to supply him with his daily ration of bread encounters Antony. The raven on this occasion provides a full loaf for the two ascetics who contest their worthiness in humility forwarding each other to break bread; they finally agree to hold each end of the loaf and act jointly.

In his *Life of St. Columba* Adomnán describes a unique rite where the saint and a bishop (who had concealed his identity) break the Eucharistic host jointly as celebrants at Iona; its isolated occurrence is a matter for conjecture. The meeting of Paul and Antony, frequent in Irish High Cross iconography, depicts both sitting or standing and with or without the incident of their breaking of the bread. Four

---

[44] See Saxl (1943; repr. 1945), Schapiro (1944), and Farrell (1987), pp. 96-117.

[45] For a comprehensive analysis of this panel, see Raw (1990), and Meyvaert in Cassidy (1992), pp. 140-5. Refer to Cassiodorus in *CCSL*: 97, pp. 406-7.

[46] See Meyvaert in Cassidy (1992), pp. 129-30, and Henderson (1985), p. 7. An edition of *The Martyrology of Oengus* is in Stokes (1905; repr. 1984).

bread. Four Paul and Antony representations have been determined for Pictish cross-slabs. On the upper triangular fragment of the Pictish Nigg slab the raven dives dramatically perpendicular to a small table, its beak pertinently bearing a loaf. Two flanking attendants, possibly deacons who were the bearers of the books of the altar to which they served, bow with books at the table's edges with dogs/lions squatting servile under their heads. The perception that this loaf lacks a segment from its lower left quarter has been deduced significant of the practice of *commixtio* in the canon of the mass, i.e. when a fragment from the host was broken and mingled with the wine which had also been consecrated. In the eighth-century Irish Stowe Missal a vernacular tract on the mass (an eleventh-century addition to the manuscript though linguistically earlier) specifies the celebrant's role in the breaking of this particle as a re-enactment of Longinus's role at Calvary.[47]

Panel Four: Christ upon the Beasts

This panel is a theophany, a revealing of divinity, which also occurs on the Bewcastle Shaft. Christ, on the largest panel on the cross, raises His right hand in benediction and holds a scroll in His left. The disjointed inscription which surrounds the panel on the Ruthwell Cross paraphrases Ps 90(91):13 ('You shall tread upon the asp and the viper; you shall trample down the lion and the dragon'). However, the beasts in the Ruthwell depiction, quadrupeds with their paws crossed, are identical and unidentified.

Meyvaert emphasizes the pacifism of the fawning beasts. He notes Cummian, Irish abbot of Clonfert, in his early seventh-century commentary on the placid compliance of the wild animals. This is likely to have been influenced by the Pseudo-Matthew's Latin commentary on Mk 1:13. The Pseudo-Matthew exposition reflects the general sense of the words of the Ruthwell inscription that surrounds the panel.

Ó Carragáin perceives the scene as polyvalent. He determines a composite conflation between the Canticle of Habakkuk (Hb 3:1-19) and Ps 90(91):13. [48] The Old Latin version of the Canticle of Habakkuk was sung every Friday for the period at lauds (dawn service of prayers) by monastic communities. Responsories based on its opening verses were also sung during the solemn ceremony of the Good Friday services that were performed at the ninth hour (3 pm). St. Jerome (*circa* AD 394) interpreted the scriptural phrase in Old Latin *in medio duorum animalium innotesceris* ('in the midst of two beasts you shall be known') (Hb 3:3) as significant of the crucified Christ being revealed between two thieves. Bede relates this to the Transfiguration (Mt 17:1-8; Mk 2:8; Lk 9:28-36) and associates it with 25 March.

Panel Five: *Agnus Dei*

Ó Carragáin lists four possibilities for the significance of the *Agnus Dei*: (a) symbolic of a prayer for private devotion used *circa* AD 700, (b) symbolic of the baptism of Christ in Scripture where John the Baptist recognizes Christ as the Lamb of God (Jn 1:28), (c) symbolic of the breaking of the bread for distribution and germane to the conclusion of the liturgical communion rite, and (d) symbolic in eschatology of the Book of Revelations, the Apocalypse of St. John which presents the Lamb of God enthroned and revered by elders and beasts. Meyvaert considers possibility (d) as most significant to the art. The nimbed figure holding the Lamb of God and standing on paired globes has been widely accepted as John the Baptist. This iconographic panel is also represented midway on the face of the Bewcastle Shaft.[49]

---

[47] On the meaning and interpretation of the Paul and Antony panel, see Ó Carragáin (1988). For a comprehensive introduction to medieval monasticism, see Lawrence (1984; repr. 1989).

[48] See Meyvaert in Cassidy (1992), pp. 125-9. Cummian's commentary on the Gospel of St. Mark is in *PL*: XXX. 594-5; the Pseudo-Augustine commentary is in *PL*: XXXV. 2149-2200. On interpreting the conflation between Ps. 90 (91):13 and the Canticle of Habakkuk, see Ó Carragáin (1986), pp. 376-403.

[49] On the four possibilities for the interpretation of the panel, see Ó Carragáin (1986), pp. 391-2. On its interpretation as an apocalyptic vision, see Meyvaert in Cassidy (1992), pp. 112-25.

Panel Six: Matthew and the Man

Interpretations for this panel remain speculative. It may represent the first of the Four Evangelists, Matthew facing his pictorial significance, the man. Early exegetical excursus on the Four Evangelists which Irenaeus (*circa* AD 140-200) and Jerome formulated based on the vision of Ezekiel (Ez 1:4-26) readily relayed itself into pictorial portrayal: Matthew the Man, Mark the Lion, Luke the Calf, and John the Eagle. Gregory the Great associates these allegorical anthropomorphisms with the beginnings of the Four Gospels, and each creature with Christ Himself; in birth a man, in death a bull, in resurrection a lion, and in ascension an eagle. In readjustment (I) on the Ruthwell Cross the eagle with St. John would be directly reflected above the transom. In this case, the Four Gospels would then have been symbolically complete if the calf and the lion had been depicted on the now lost right and left arms of the cross-beam.[50]

Panel Seven: The Eagle

The eagle situated above the cross centre holds a sprig in its talons, evidentially of the vine. In readjustment (I) this would appear on the opposite East (now South) face above the archer. The image of the eagle was common in early Christian art as a symbol of victory and resurrection, and its flight reflective of Christ's Ascension. Gregory the Great in his patristic excursus *Moralia* in Job demonstrates how the eagle could imply various significances: (a) the malign spirits that decimate souls (Lam 4:19); (b) earthly kings (Ez 17:3-4) and divinity who on descending to earth incarnate ascends and soars again to the heavens above. Meyvaert stresses Gregory's allusions within this text to a metaphorical focus on monastic contemplation.[51]

A Summary of the Latin Inscriptions

The Ruthwell Cross series of Latin inscriptions are the most extensive in early Anglo-Latin. Yet they are syntactically incomplete, condensed, and contracted. Their lateral encompassment of the iconographic panels greatly substantiates and directs our comprehension of the sculpted depictions but does not secure the arrangement, allegorical or full polyvalent implications. In the transcription of the engraved Latin inscriptions conventional palaeographical rules are adhered to, following Okasha (1971).[52]

East (now South) Face

Panel 2	Annunciation
Top:	*INGRESSVSA[NG]-*
Panel 3	The Healing of the Man Born Blind
Top:	*+ETPRAETERIENS:VIDI[...]T[...]R[...]*
Right:	*ANATIBITATE:ETS[...]*
Panel 4	Mary Anoints Christ's Feet
Top:	*+A[..V.......]B[.]*
Right:	*STRVM:V[NGVE]NTI:&S[T]AN[SR]E[TR]OSECVSPEDES*
Left:	*EIVSLACRIMIS:C/OEPITRIGARE:PEDESIVS:&CAPILLIS:*
Bottom:	*CAPITISSVITERGEBAT*
Panel 5	Martha & Mary/Visitation
	damaged runic inscription, but the runic letters for 'Martha' and a possible 'M' are decipherable.

---

[50] For Gregory the Great's commentary see *PL*: LXX, esp. *PL*: LXX. 625.
[51] See Meyvaert in Cassidy (1992), pp. 145-7. See Moralia XXXI, Nos. 94-104 in *CCSL*: 143B.1614-1623.
[52] For a discussion of these Latin inscriptions, see Howlett in Cassidy (1992), pp. 72-82.

| Panel 6 | The Archer |
| | eroded and indecipherable. |

| Panel 7 | The Man and the Eagle |
| | eroded and indecipherable. |

West (now North) Face

Panel 2	The Flight Into/Out of Egypt
Top:	+MARIA:ETIO[.....]
Left:	TV[O...]

Panel 3	Paul and Antony
Top:	+SCS:PAVLVS:
Right:	ET:A[...]
Left:	FREGER[..T]:PANEMINDESERTO:

Panel 4	Christ upon the Beasts
Top:	[.]IHSX[.S]
Left:	IVD[.]X[..]EQV[IT]A[TI]S:
Right:	BESTIAE:ET:DRACON[ES]:COGNOUERVNT:INDE:

Panel 5	*Agnus Dei*
Top:	-DORAMUS
Bottom:	TNONEVM

| Panel 6 | Matthew and the Man |
| | eroded and indecipherable. |

| Panel 7 | The Eagle |
| | indecipherable runic inscription. |

The Dream of the Rood

The text of *The Dream of the Rood* along with other legendary, homiletic, and poetic material is to be found in Vercelli, Biblioteca Capitolare, MS CXVII, more generally known as the Vercelli Book.[1] It is now in the care of the Cathedral Library at Vercelli in northern Italy. The town of Vercelli was founded by the Romans *circa* AD 361, and became renowned as a station for pilgrims from northern and central Europe as they made their way towards the centre of Christendom, Rome.[2]

The manuscript itself is well preserved. It comprises of 136 regular-sized parchment folios made from sheepskin. Each folio measures *circa* 31 cm by 20 cm. They are grouped into gatherings that are numbered from I – XIX at the top of every folio and by the letters A – T at the bottom of the final folio in each gathering. It is a plain text manuscript with no decorative artistic pages or space-provision made for illumination; in fact, it contains only a few ornate initial letters. All the folios have been ruled for between 23 and 33 lines of writing with the number of lines to each page similar within each gathering.

The scribal hand throughout the complete codex is regular and legible. The script used is an insular quadratic Anglo-Saxon miniscule, which is indicative of late tenth-century West-Saxon scriptoria. The Vercelli Book is normally dated by scholars to the end of the tenth century or the beginning of the eleventh; M. Förster's proposed dating to the latter part of the tenth century scholars now generally accept to be the most plausible.[3]

The linguistic features of the Vercelli Book provide little specific evidence as to its dating or history. Few special traits are common throughout the manuscript. Anglian and Kentish distinctive forms occur frequently in late West-Saxon texts; yet they appear in too arbitrary a manner for any objective conclusions to be made. Several extant manuscripts copied at scriptoria in Canterbury and Rochester contain versions of Vercelli homilies and sermons.[4] A Kentish influence in the Vercelli Book is the constant use of the abbreviation xb, a contraction most common in late tenth-century manuscripts emanating from Canterbury.[5] Palaeographers have demonstrated that the knot-words on the initials in fols. 49rv, 106v, and 112rv are indicative of types in earlier tenth-century manuscripts from scriptoria at Winchester.[6] Such evidence seems to indicate therefore that the Vercelli Book was a product of one of these scriptoria in the South-east.

There has been much speculation and debate as to why and how this plain Anglo-Saxon codex came to be in Vercelli. Illuminated manuscripts from England were highly prized objects in mainland Europe during the early Middle Ages; this codex is not, however, of such quality. The only documents that contained Anglo-Saxon south of the Italian Alps during the medieval period were fragments that most likely came from individual bindings, which tends to indicate that they were dispatched to the region soon after their completion in England.

Scribal evidence confirms that the manuscript was still in England at the beginning of the eleventh century. K. Sisam suggests that the words 'writ þus' at the bottom of fol. 63v and 'sclean' on fol. 99r signify that the manuscript was not destined to be transported overseas at that time.[7] By the end of the eleventh century, however, the book was at Vercelli. In the blank space at the end of fol. 24v a later hand transcribed a variation in the music of an Italian church service. It is an extract from Psalm 26 written in small Carolingian miniscule with musical notation that is typical of north Italian scribes *circa* AD 1100.[8]

As a result of this scribal evidence, certain theories concerning the history of the Vercelli Book can be disregarded; the arguments are based on dates that are too late in time. As cited, the town of

---

[1] A facsimile of the manuscript is in Sisam (1976).
[2] For further details on Vercelli, see Swanton (1987; repr. 1992), pp. 1-4.
[3] Förster (1913), pp. 11-21. See also Hoops (1911-9), p. 102, Keller (1906), p. 106, and Wülcker (1894), p. vii.
[4] See Scragg (1973), p. 207.
[5] Sisam (1953), pp. 109-10.
[6] Decorated initials in English manuscripts are discussed in Wormald (1945), pp. 120, 134.
[7] Sisam (1913), pp. 305-10, and Sisam (1953), p. 113.
[8] See Sisam (1953), pp. 113-15. For further discussion on the Italian connection, refer to Ó Carragáin (1998).

Vercelli functioned as a stop-off point for pilgrims travelling between Anglo-Saxon England and Rome, and the presence of its *Hospitalis Scottum* dates from before the beginning of the twelfth century. It is plausible that the manuscript may have been in the baggage of an important English palmer taking this route to Rome in the twelfth century. Another possibility is that it may have come indirectly to Vercelli via a monastery like Fulda or Fluery, which had close connections with England. Historically, the codex most likely arrived at Vercelli during the latter part of the eleventh century since the monastery diminished in significance after that time.[9]

The Vercelli Book contains twenty-three Old English homilies and sermons.[10] The texts begin with treatises on Christ's Passion and Final Judgement (fols. 1r – 12v), and go on to works dealing with various kinds of immoral behaviour such as the vices of licentiousness and intemperance. The final prose piece is a version of the Life of St. Guthlac (fols. 133v – 135v). The manuscript arrangement conforms loosely around particular themes. This suggests that the compiler and/or scribes were drawing on material from several sources and not assigning any premeditated structure or sequence apart from adhering to their own thematic plan. Interspersed through these prose texts are six verse pieces of differing lengths. The longest of these are *Andreas* and *The Fates of the Apostles* (fols. 29v – 54r), which are poems on Christian evangelization. These are proceeded later in the manuscript at fols. 101v – 106v by two poetic fragments which G. P. Krapp terms as *Body & Soul I* and *Homiletic Fragment I,* and by *The Dream of the Rood.* The final poetic text is *Elene* (fols. 121r – 133v). This is a verse rendering of the legend of St. Helena's finding of the True Cross near the site of Christ's execution in Jerusalem, and is directly connected to the content of *The Dream.*[11]

The Dream of the Rood begins at the sixth line of fol. 104v and concludes at the end of fol. 106r. This places the text at the end of gathering XIV (concluding at fol. 104v) which is ruled for twenty-four lines per page, and at the beginning of gathering XV (commencing at fol. 105r) which is ruled for thirty-two lines per page. The text is the product of one scribal hand, written in regular and uniform insular quadratic Anglo-Saxon miniscule script. The punctuation changes at the beginning of gathering XV reflect the narrower ruling of the pages in this quire. The text of the poem begins with two majuscule letters 'H' and 'Þ', but such lettering is rare throughout. M. Swanton argues that majuscule lettering is used in the poems in the Vercelli Book as a guide to rhythm and emphasis rather than syntax. The most common occurrences are 'Ac' and 'Hwæðe'; these signify the opening of clauses or sentences that present central themes and images. Yet it should be noted that such use is neither consistent nor regular throughout the codex.

This is particularly true of the text of *The Dream,* where punctuation is employed sporadically, and mainly for syntactical reasons. In ll. 22-25 of fol. 105r, however, the scribe has regularly pointed the text after each half-line (except after 'licgende', l. 24).[12] This indicates a possible experiment in metrical punctuation, but for the remainder of the poem this practice is discontinued with punctuation patterns reverting to being syntactical and irregular. The symbol ': ,' after 'gesceaft' (l. 12) and 'treow' (l. 17), and its variant ': ~' which ends the poem, is normally used, as is the case throughout the Vercelli Book, to indicate the end of a particular section. The employment of punctuation in the poem is capricious and variable from which no congruent patterns can be observed.

The Dream of the Rood is written in typical late West Saxon but certain non-West-Saxon forms exist in the poem. Some scholars have argued that these forms may present linguistic evidence indicating the historical transmission of the text.[13] This view is untenable as evidence can only conclusively highlight mixed poetic rather than dialectal word-usage.[14] Furthermore, a reliance mainly

---

[9] On the background, providence, and history of the Vercelli Book, see Borgognone (1951), Clayton (1985), Cook (1888), de Grégory (1819-24), Förster (1913), Halsall (1969), Herben (1935), Ó Carragáin (1975), and Scragg (1973).

[10] On the compilation of the Vercelli Book, see Scragg (1973), esp. pp. 206-7; the Vercelli Homilies are edited in Scragg (1992), and the content of the manuscript is outlined in Table 3, pp. 94-5.

[11] The poems of the Vercelli Book are edited in Krapp (1932).

[12] See Krapp (1932), pp. xxviii-xxxi.

[13] See Brunner (1965), esp. §§ 107, 214, & 425, Campbell (1959), §§ 222-3, 446, & 579, and Swanton (1987; repr. 1992), p. 49.

[14] See the discussion in Sisam (1953), pp. 119-39.

on vocabulary to ascertain the dialectical origins of Old English verse would prove inconclusive.[15] Poetic vocabulary in Anglo-Saxon usually contains elements from other dialects such as Anglian, Kentish, and Northumbrian.[16] What then is the significance of this? These dialectic words demonstrate vestiges of scribal tradition (continuity) which is realized in the copying of the material into the Vercelli manuscript, and of scribal changes (discontinuity), which are manifested by errors, dialectic changes, modifications, etc., in the act of copying itself. Instances of Anglian words in the poem are 'sceððan' (l. 47), 'gefringan' (ll. 76, 112), and 'bearn' (l. 83).[17] The second part of the place-name 'feorgbold' (l. 73) is also typically Anglian; 'boðl' is its Northumbrian form, and 'bold' with metathesis is chiefly Mercian.[18] The past participle suffix -ad rather than -od in the verb 'geniwian' (l. 148) is a typical Kentish form; it is also on occasions used in Anglian.[19] The word 'bestemed' (ll. 22 & 48) is from the Northumbrian rendering on the Ruthwell Cross, and also recurs in the late West Saxon inscription on the Brussels Cross.[20] To conclude, the linguistic character of *The Dream* simply adheres to the standard literary language in use towards the end of the Anglo-Saxon period, late West Saxon with an Anglian element as well as traces from other dialects. The use of the vernacular, if presented orally, would ultimately encompass all audiences.[21]

The beginning of the poem can be divided into two parts. The first part (ll. 4-12) presents the universal perimeters of the Cross-vision. Here the gold-covered and gem-studded Cross is portrayed and described, culminating in the dreamer's acknowledgement that this is an eschatological Cross, 'Ne wæs ðær huru fracodes gealga' (l. 10b). The second part (ll. 13-23) focuses on presenting the dreamer as a sinful member of humankind, within the context of this all-encompassing Cross.[22] The poet in a subtle use of the word 'fah' (l. 13.) capitulates an ambiguity signifying both stained with sins (the dreamer) and brightly coloured (the Cross). At l. 18 an important shift in tone occurs. Introduced by the conjunction 'hwæðre', the Cross-vision begins to sweat on the right side and the dreamer becomes overcome by sorrow and fear. As he anxiously observes this ever-changing beam and beacon for a prolonged time, it must, among other things, conjure up for him thoughts of Christ's Second Coming (*Parousia*) and the Day of Judgement – the time when his temporal life will be evaluated according to its merits and demerits.[23]

The Cross begins to prepare to speak directly to the dreamer from l. 24, which is once more introduced by the conjunctive adverb 'hwæðe'.[24] The Cross commences speaking at l. 28 by distancing between its participation in the historical act of the Crucifixion and its present state of glory. A certain tension is manifest when it recalls the forceful manner in which it was removed from the edge of the forest and positioned on the hill as an object of execution. This anxiety intensifies as the Cross recalls the sight of Christ as a hero running to mount it. It even expresses doubt that it may be capable of the important task of supporting Christ in His realization of the Paschal event. The impact of this exposé derives from the paradox that the Cross, which was once the embodiment of death, is now a means by which believers, including the dreamer, are challenged to come to seek eternal life.

The scene of Christ resolutely running to the Cross differs from the biblical accounts of the Passion, which depict Christ as a tortured and exhausted figure personally carrying His Cross to the place of execution. This shift in emphasis displays the astuteness of the Anglo-Saxon poet to

---

[15] Sisam (1953), pp. 126-31.

[16] On dialectic forms, see Hedberg (1945), Sievers (1885), pp. 464-5, and Sisam (1953), pp. 123-5.

[17] Jordan (1906), pp. 43-4, 94-7, 107.

[18] Ekwall (1917), pp. 82-91, and Smith (1956), I, p. 44, ii, map 8.

[19] Brunner (1965), § 414.

[20] Swanton (1987; repr. 1992), p. 49.

[21] On audience, see the discussion in Fleming (1966), and Ó Carragáin (1987-88) & (1992). While it is generally accepted that the poem engenders monastic spirituality, the fact that it was composed in the vernacular its meaning would have been accessible even to those without a proficiency in Latin. This group would include lay monks.

[22] See the discussion on this section of the poem in Patten (1968), and Raw (1970).

[23] Hieatt (1971) notices verbal and thematic echoes in the opening and closing parts of the poem. See also Kintgen (1974).

[24] On the use of such conjunctive adverbs in *The Dream*, see the discussion in Bolton (1959-60).

culturally tailor his subject-matter for his audience. Anglo-Saxon society valued strong and brave heroes who were assisted by loyal and worthy thanes. The epic poem *Beowulf*, for instance, continually presents this theme, which is especially highlighted in the relationship between the hero, Beowulf, and his thane, Wiglaf, towards the climax of the poem. The relationship between Christ and the Cross is viewed in similar terms in *The Dream*.

The poet establishes a very effective contrast between the intransigence of the human characters and the willingness of the inanimate Cross to accept Christ. The living tree (Rood) now turned gallows emphasizes Christ's desire to mount it and its need to be steadfast in the face of this command.[25] The image of the Cross trembling at l. 42 as Christ mounts highlights the magnanimity of the task it has undertaken, 'Bifode ic þa me se beorn ymbclypte'. In unison with Christ it expresses the suffering inflicted by their mutual opponents.

The poet presents the Cross as the most elite inanimate object of all lifeless things, elevates it to the dramatic cynosure, and imbues it with the power of speech through the convention of the dream vision. Consequentially it came to be honoured as the noblest of woods on the hill (ll. 90-1). In the Crucifixion event, emphasis is placed on the nails driven into the wood, the poignant open wounds, the Cross's inability to harm its enemies, and its being drenched with blood from Christ's side. The Cross is not depicted as bleeding or expressing fear or pain. Rather as a witness it subjectively retells the events endured on the hill in terms of violence and derision that were directed against Christ when, as His loyal thane, it endured the death of the Saviour.[26]

Scholars who directly attribute human emotions to the Rood tend to misinterpret the context of the situation where it merely reports what it witnessed on the first Good Friday. Its only autonomously willed action is when it gently presents the body of the dead Christ into the hands of friends. It stands there bloody and scarred during Christ's entombment until its own eventual burial, lamenting with the other two crosses, as all creation did, the death of its king.

The Cross's distress is apparent after the Crucifixion; yet the repetition of the connective 'hwæðre' at l. 57a, l. 70a and l. 75b projects the narrative forward. Christ is at rest in the tomb, the physical body is cooling; further elaboration is neither necessary nor required. Introduced by the adverb 'nu' at l. 78, the contemporary Cross quickly reasserts it role in the redemptive event, and does not at any time throughout the entire poem equate itself with the dreamer or humanity. Its shared experience with Christ symbolically permits it to represent Him as a healing agent and teacher.[27] The vision of the Cross towering high in the heavens is because God's Son penetrated the very centre of darkness and death, hell, and conquered it in triumph, restoring light and life; this is termed as the Harrowing of Hell.[28]

The Rood's deliberation moves quickly to the present tense as it reveals its changed status. An obvious sense of triumph emanates from the vision, which is in sharp contrast to its account of its historical role. The Cross is now emphasizing its glorified, contemporary status as a healing agent and representative symbol of Christ. The poet effectively asserts this paradox of status in a very effective 'then/now' passage at ll. 80b-94, where Christ's humiliating death is dealt with in a single line, 'On me Bearn Godes þrowode hwile'(ll. 83b-84a), as the basis for the Cross's present exalted status.

It is also noteworthy that in the section which focuses on the Crucifixion scene (ll. 28-75a) the person of Christ is referred to in human terms only four or five times, while the words signifying Him as God are present eleven or twelve times. As man Christ endured death on the Cross and sent forth His spirit in the act of dying as revelation had determined. As God He rose from the dead and realized the possibility of eternal life for mankind; in fact, the Crucifixion is perceived as a victory from the very beginning of the poem, especially from l. 13.

In the central part of the poem the dreamer receives instruction from the Cross on the doctrinal message that he is to promulgate to the faithful. The interpretative importance of the Crucifixion is maintained throughout this sermonizing section. Christ is the Son of God (l. 83b), Prince of Glory (l.

---

[25] For further elaboration on this point, see Gardner (1971; repr. 1983), p. 149.

[26] See Orton (1980), pp. 2-3, for a discussion on the Riddle genre and *The Dream of the Rood*; see also Swanton (1987; repr. 1992), pp. 66-7.

[27] Huppé (1970), p. 101.

[28] Irving (1986), p. 110.

90b), Guardian of Heaven (l. 91b), Lord (l. 105b), and Saviour (l. 111b). He is also the One who freed mankind both from personal wrongdoing and from Original Sin as instigated by Adam (ll. 98-100). These titles referring to the risen Christ are similar to those used in the depiction of the Crucifixion scene itself, except that there His assumed humanity and sufferings had to be acknowledged. The emotional image of the mutilated tree (ll. 39-56), superceded as a symbol of redemption (ll. 84b-85a) functions as an effective doctrinal lesson from l. 95. The dreamer undergoes a *metanoia* ('a change of heart') as a result of being a witness in his dream to this vision. It is highly significant that he has the sole responsibility as the role of 'reordberend' ('voice-bearer') for the Cross, and is urged to convey to the faithful the message and means of redemption that has been revealed to him through the dream-vision. The Cross, therefore, as inanimate object is not depicted as speaking directly to mankind except through the persona of the dreamer.

The device of the Cross speaking, changing from gem-studded object plated with gold through which is seen the vista of the past, to severed forest tree, to gallows, to glorified Rood, and, ultimately, as the means to Christ and the possibility of eternal life. All these phenomena constitute the essence of reverie and of effective teaching.[29] The Crucifixion remains central to the Cross's contemporary status, and almost half of the poem (sixty-five lines) focuses mainly on the tree as object of death. While the Passion is the central part of the Good Friday liturgy, the wider eschatological theme of the poem encourages the repentance (*metanoia*) of the faithful before an impending Day of Judgement. The Rood now acquires the tone of a preacher and represents a notable shift from the proclamation style of the preceding lines, or the emotional impact of the opening section. Repeating the homiletic formula 'hæleð min se leofa' of l. 78, it now instructs the dreamer (ll. 95-109) to reveal to mankind the supernatural symbolic vision that he has just witnessed and to present it in the context of the Creed (*Credo*), the ecclesiastical proclamation of belief.

Throughout the entire poem, the poet does not dwell much on the fear associated with the Day of Judgement, emphasizing instead the inevitable fulfilment of Christ's redemptive sacrifice. The overall treatment of this theme is positive. In answer to the poignant question as to whether one's life has been predominantly good or evil which the Lord will judge, only a few souls, the poet reminds us, will find anything to utter in reply. However, he goes on to inform at ll. 118-19 that no one need be afraid who has before that day the sign of the Rood on his or her chest. The universality of this instruction is emphasized in the proceeding passage (ll. 119-21) where it is explained that by means of the Cross each believer may seek eternal life. In contrast to the dreamer who appeared terrified at the first sight of the Cross-vision but later was reprieved to recount the message of redemption, Christians at Doomsday must have the symbol of the Cross on their breast in order to be accredited with the gift of salvation. Medieval anticipations of the termination of all reverberate here.[30]

The physical existence of Christ is affirmed through the differing perspectives of the person and function of Mary, the Mother of Christ. The similarity is striking between Mary and the Rood in that both are obedient servants and revered agents of Christ as well as being approachable mediums of salvation; the Rood itself makes this parallel at ll. 90-4; their interrelated role has a further significance because it symbolically associates the Annunciation with the Crucifixion. According to tradition Christ is presumed to have died in the same day that He was conceived which is 25 March, the Feast of the Annunciation, the day of the spring equinox when day and night, represented by the sun and moon, are of equal length. Light increases after this date, making it a profound metaphor for Christ's victory over death.

The poet accepts without comment the death on the Cross of the man who was also divine.[31] He conveys the paradox of death and life solely through experiences recounted by the authoritative cult image of the Cross. The appropriate connection between suffering and glory is depicted in the exalted symbolic vision of the Rood, not in the passively enduring gallows. The reference to Adam's ancient deeds at l. 100 recalls a depth of biblical and liturgical tradition since Christ is frequently interpreted

---

[29] See the discussion in Edwards (1970), esp. pp. 293, 301.

[30] The Blickling text for Easter Day, edited in Morris (1874, 1876, 1880; repr. 1967), pp. 82-96, advises its listeners in a similar way with regard to the Second Coming of Christ.

[31] On moral authority in Old English verse, see Shippey (1972), esp. pp. 70-1.

as the second Adam who undid the negative transgressions of the first Adam. Following the way of the Cross, it is from death comes life and from despair springs hope.

At the poem's climax (ll.126b-44a), the dreamer embarks on a proper devotion to the victory-tree, honouring it, as men do throughout time and creation (l. 12, l. 82), together with a handful of followers (ll. 123b-24a). The emphasis is on prayer, devotion, and focusing the mind (*meditatio*) on the Cross as the means to Christ and to His gift of salvation. This otherworldly longing is replaced at the very end of the poem (ll. 144b-54) by a form of incantation that distinguishes the authoritative perception of Christ's redeeming act from the dreamer's appropriate response to the vision that he has experienced. It becomes a prayer of petition where the dreamer may be made a welcomed guest at heaven's feast (ll.135a-41). He may then be among the multitude that Christ as Saviour has and shall lead to God's kingdom, as a consequence of His sacrifice on the Cross (ll. 142-44a). The two final lines of the poem (ll. 155-6) equate Christ with God. This effectively reminds us of the opening of the poem because the Cross was first introduced as a glorified and eschatological symbol. The audience is finally left with the enduring image of the eschatological Christ residing over heaven and earth – all creation – in a spirit of triumph and fairness.[32]

The purpose of this introduction to the poem is neither to diminish nor ignore the literal structure of the text; nor to apply a too subtle, symbolic, or figurative overview; nor isolate theological abstractions in a few designated passages. Adherence to a sense of thematic and structural balance helps focus on *The Dream of the Rood's* central purpose: objectively and subjectively to inform. The poem imaginatively presents a living belief as practiced; for the most part it avoids elaborating on abstract theological ideologies. Rather it displays a tangible insight into the mystery of the Incarnation-Atonement by presenting it in terms of perceptible acts of mercy in the process of God's revelation to mankind through history. These divine interventions, which the Cross in its admonitory passage (ll. 95-121) instructs the dreamer, are to be acknowledged with gratitude, atonement and praise, and as being ultimately beyond human understanding. Through the Cross-vision, the goal of the dreamer's experience is to guide believers in the ways of salvation before the impending Doomsday.

---

[32] Garde (1991), pp. 90-112, provides interesting insights into *The Dream of the Rood*, both thematically and textually.

The Processional Cross and Cross Reliquary

Procession, the intended movement of a group of people from place to place for specific religious motives, was practiced widely in pre-Christian times. In the biblical Old Testament procession implies the pilgrimage of a people, the Israelites, in the company of God. In the New Testament the faithful follow Christ to listen to His teachings and later to commemorate His Death and Resurrection.[1]

In the Old Testament the Ark of the Covenant was carried in procession. The ark symbolized the presence of Yahweh and of His covenant with Israel; it contained two tablets of stone thought to originate from the Mosaic period (1K 8:9). It was also believed to contain the rod of Aaron, father of the Judaic priesthood, and a vessel of manna. It was placed to rest finally in the temple of Solomon (1K 8:6). In the New Testament it is described as the heavenly temple (Heb 9:4; Apc 11:19), a typological prefigurement of the Christian Church.[2]

Procession gradually became more extensive through the early Christian liturgical year.[3] The disciples bore palm fronds at Jesus's entry into Jerusalem (Jn 12:13); by the fourth century palms were carried in procession in Jerusalem during Holy Week, in Spain by the sixth, and in France by the ninth. In the late fourth century the Pilgrimage of Egeria account describes at firsthand sacred sites visited in Jerusalem by pilgrims and worshippers during Holy Week. Stational Church feasts were undertaken from the fifth century onwards which entailed processional liturgical celebrations stopping at particular churches dedicated to early martyrs. The *Ordo Romanus Primus* describes the pontifical stational masses in seventh-century Rome. By the end of the seventh century, Marian devotions originating in Byzantium began to flourish in Rome: crosses were carried and held in procession at Christmas, the Annunciation, Purification, and Marian Dormition. By the eighth century the processional ritual of the translation of saints' relics became a well-established practice. Funeral rites too were processional. Crosses were also carried in procession during times of crisis. Pope Gregory the Great (AD 540-604) attests to the early procession with crosses through the streets of Rome to supplicate for protection against plague.

During the liturgy of the mass both gospel and offertory processions were undertaken; in the Medieval Church these proceeded from the chancel which was screened in its sanctity from the congregation. Processions not only included the bearing of the Cross but lights or candles, the colour of vestments and banners, incense and relics. The acolyte, a minor order of the ministry of the Church, was invested with ceremonial functions, which included the bearing of ceremonial lights. The deacon, a minister of the major ecclesiastical orders, was invested with the prominent liturgical role (among others) of the bearing of the Gospel Book and the reading of its lessons (pericopes); he also attended to the altar and its rites during mass.

At Easter and Pentecost processions were undertaken to the font for baptism. From an early period in the Church the consecrated Eucharistic host came to be reserved. In a liturgical service known as the presanctified mass the host was carried in procession by the officiating deacon for its distribution to the assembled faithful at the communion rite.[4] In the Byzantine rite the Eucharist was not celebrated during Lent excepting Saturdays and Sundays which were non-fasting days. In the Western Church the consecrated Eucharist was specially reserved at the evening mass of the Last Supper on Holy (Maundy) Thursday. At the end of this service it was carried behind the processional cross to an altar of repose for distribution the following day during the services of Good Friday.

Rogation Days were days of intercession and prayer and were very popular in the Medieval Church with some occurring annually and others being arranged to suit local needs.[5] Only four such days have been universally observed for many centuries: April 25 and the three days preceding Ascension Day. April 25 was chosen to replace with a Christian procession the pagan *Robigalia*

---

[1] See the discussion on procession by Jasper in Davies (1972; repr. 1978), pp. 323-4. See also Andrieu (1931-61), Dunlop (1932), Frere (1906), & Henderson (1882).

[2] On the Ark of Covenant see McKenzie (1966; repr. 1975), pp. 54-55.

[3] On the development of the liturgical year, see Talley (1986).

[4] On the presanctified mass, see Jardine Grisbrooke in Davies (1972; repr. 1978), pp. 322-3.

[5] On the Rogation Days, see Connelly in Davies (1972; repr. 1978), pp. 336-7.

processions of that date. As this always occurred in the Easter season, it was not a fast day and the procession was festal, similar to the processions that took place during Easter week. During *Robigalia* the gods were implored to preserve the crops from mildew and other diseases; the Christian adoption of this festival preserved this meaning. The faithful filed in procession around the fields to invoke God's blessing on the crops.

An important feature of Rogation Days is the singing in procession of the litanies of the saints. April 25 is known as the greater Litanies and the other three as the lesser. The Litanies used are the same on all four days. Such liturgical processions from the fourth century onwards were generally proceeded by a processional cross that was the decorative symbol of triumph. The Anglo-Saxon Brussels Cross (Plate IX, p. 34) and The Rupertus Cross (Plate XXIII, p. 75) are examples of decorative crosses that could have functioned as processional crosses and/or shrines that contained fragments of the True Cross. The Anglo-Saxon Church observed the Rogation days, especially those three preceding Ascension, with particular reverence. The Blickling Homilies, the Vercelli Book, and Ælfric's Catholic Homilies, Series I & II, all provide preaching texts for these days.[6]

Other liturgical celebrations which embodied the procession of the Cross were Ember Days which included the Wednesday, Friday and Saturday of three and then later four weeks in the year.[7] Ember weeks, like Lent, were occasions of spiritual renewal, times of prayer and fasting originally coincidental with the Roman seasons of sowing, harvest, and grape-gathering. The Old Roman Missal, *circa* tenth century, assigns six or twelve lection passages at different times for the Ember vigil; this was similar to the Easter vigil.

Anglo-Saxon crosses and crucifixes were engaged in religious processions and/or were enshrined as reliquaries with fragments of the True Cross. They would have held place either within the inner sanctum of the veiled chancel or in ancillary chapels within the church. In later periods they may have been placed above the high altar or on a nearby beam. Some were carved of wood. Others were formed of precious metals, and many were jewelled. The historical references can prove ambiguous: both Latin and Old English use the same word (*crux* and *rod*) for both Cross and Crucifix (i.e. a figural representation) without differentiation. By the seventh century Aldhelm describes a cross that was decorated with gold, gems, and silver. In the eighth Alcuin refers to crosses gilded with gold and silver at York. King Cnut presented a large, sanctified and ornamented cross to New Minster at Winchester. At times our evidence for the Anglo-Saxon jewelled cross and crucifix is contingent on references to the spoils carried off by invaders. After the Norman Conquest of AD 1066, Hereward and his raiders had no fewer than fifteen crosses or crucifixes seized from Peterborough. Other wealthy monasteries were documented to include large numbers of crosses or crucifixes: three gold crosses and six silver at Waltham, twenty-six at Glastonbury (AD 1045), and twenty-seven at Ely by the time of the Conquest. Monastic churches received crucifixes that were donated by secular patrons. King Eadred bequeathed two gold crucifixes to Old Minster at Winchester; Earl Bryhtnoth presented two more (or crosses) to Ely. A lady, Ælfwaru, wishing to be buried at Ely bestowed a further two representations on the establishment.

Crosses or crucifixes could achieve large proportions with more affluent monasteries and churches sponsoring, commissioning, or possessing life-size representations of the figure of Christ. None now exist yet records maintain that a silver-plated crucifix donated by Stigand to Ely was according to human scale as reputedly was one set over the altar at Bury. Often their Crucifixion scene included the Virgin and John at Christ's feet as of a crucifix given by Leofric and Godiva to Evesham before the Conquest.

The Brussels Cross

A lively interest in Cross relics was maintained well into the Anglo-Saxon period. From the early part of the twelfth century comes an important Cross-reliquary now at the Cathedral of SS. Michel-et-

---

[6] The Blickling Homiles are edited in Morris (1874, 1876, 1880; repr. 1967); the Vercelli texts are in Scragg (1992), and Ælfric's Catholic Homilies are in Godden (1979), Pope (1967-8), & Thorpe (1844-6).

[7] On the Ember Days, see Connelly in Davies (1972; repr. 1978), pp. 168-9.

Gudule in Brussels, Belgium, and popularly known as the Brussels Cross. This cross, bearing a two-line inscription in Anglo-Saxon verse, was first brought to the attention of scholars by Zupitza (after Logeman in 1891).[8] Traditionally reputed to have contained fragments of the True Cross, it has been at the Brussels Cathedral since the middle of the seventeenth century.

The cross is 46.5cm high by 28cm wide (18.3 inches by 11 inches) in size. The front and principal face was once covered by a jewelled gold plate which is now lost. This face would probably have originally depicted a Crucifixion scene. An inscription on a gilded silver plate that was attached to the foot of the cross reads: *Direpta 7Ma/Martii, Publicae/Venerationi/ Restituta/ 29Na 7Bris/1793* ('Looted 7 March, restored for public veneration 29 September 1793'). This refers to the plundering of the cross by French soldiers in 1793. The rear face is still covered by a silver plate bearing medallions depicting the four evangelist symbols, one of each on the four arms, and an *Agnus Dei* figure (Lamb with transfixing Cross) in a roundel at its centre. Across the silver plating of the transom the artist has inscribed his name: '+Drahmal me worhte'. The Anglo-Saxon inscription is incised on a silver strip that runs around the edges of the cross. It is written not in runes but in Roman letters in a curious mixture of capitals and miniscules. The letters NE of 'ricne', NG of 'cyning', and ME of 'bestemed' are written in ligatures.

It is generally accepted that the Brussels Cross is English in origin. The three brothers, Ælfric, Æthlmær, and Athelwold, referred to in the prose section of the inscription, have never been positively identified. The name of the craftsman, Drahmal, is Norse and may perhaps indicate that he originated from the northern part of Britain; nothing more is known about him.

Determining from the language of its epigraph and ornamentation the cross dates from the early twelfth century. The language is generally regular late West Saxon with one Anglian form 'bestemed', and a few irregular spellings such as 'byfigynede' (with 'y' for 'e' in the ending) in the verse, and 'wyrican' and 'beropor' (both with an intrusive vowel) in the prose. The Anglian form 'bestemed' (for West Saxon 'bestiemed', 'bestymed') does not necessarily indicate a northern origin for the inscription; it can more plausibly be explained as a traditional spelling adopted from an older poetic vocabulary.

Cook has suggested that the three names, Ælfric, Æthlmær, and Athelwold might be synonymous with Alfricus, Agelmarus, and Agelwardus, three of the six brothers of Eadric of Streona mentioned by Florence of Worcester under the year AD 1007.[9] Dickens and Ross argue that the Æthelmær of the inscription is the well-known patron of Ælfric, who founded the Abbey of Eynsham in AD 1005; they offer no identification for the two other names.[10] It is possible that this holy relic that forms part of the present cross is the same as the *lignum Domini* sent by Pope Martius to King Ælfred in AD 883 or 885. None of these possibilities can be conclusively proved. D'Ardenne, however, who favours the identification of the relic with Ælfred's *lignum Domini* has made a study of all the available evidence, presenting a plausible and accurate account of its later history. According to d'Ardenne, the relic remained in the hands of the West-Saxon royal family until near the end of the tenth century, when it left the possession of the family's direct line. The cross's new owners had it enclosed in a reliquary (the present cross) and presented to Westminister Abbey.[11] It later found its way to the Netherlands, probably during the reign of King Stephen, when Flemish soldiers were stationed in England.

In January 1999, A. van Vpersele de Strihou, Curator at the Cathedral of SS. Michel-et-Gudule in Brussels, discovered a rare document relating to the Brussels Cross within the archives of the chapter-church (now cathedral). This contains (i) a diagram of the cross, comprising of the cross inscription and a Latin translation from *circa* 1650, with an additional translation in Dutch by Prof. H. Logeman dated 1894 (Fig. 4, p. 76); and (ii) notes on the cross diagram from *circa* 1650 (Fig. 5, p. 77). She has graciously given permission to produce this document in this edition, which highlights scholarly interest in the Brussels Cross as early as *circa* 1650 and its continuance to the present time.

---

[8] Zupitza (1891), Logeman (1891). See also the discussion in Dobbie (1942), pp. cxviii, clxxiv, 115, & 204.

[9] Cook (1905), pp. ix - xvii, 3 - 5.

[10] Dickens & Ross (1934), pp. 1-13, 25-29.

[11] d'Ardenne (1939), pp. 145-64, 271-2.

Translator's Note

The Dream of the Rood is a literary poem of witness, voiced by both the dreamer and the Rood. Muffled by a millennium, the translation should strive to empathize with what has been heard and like a 'bearer of voices' (spoke of in the poem) to once more convey. Ezra Pound distinguishes between two modes of conveyance: 'interpretative translation', a rendering with which most translators comply, as of here, and the more liberal and original paraphrase. To interpret is to engage a fidelity to the text with new expression in sense and sensibility that will vary vastly in manner and degree from translator to translator. In recommendation, however, a faithfulness directing within the translation should be flexible and non-inhibitive.

King Ælfred the Great in his Preface to *St. Gregory's Pastoral Care* (AD 871-99), a translation into Anglo-Saxon of Gregory the Great's *Cura Pastoralis*, which was a standard directive model for clerical orders, explains the accommodative implications of an interpretative gap. While deploring the loss and lack of Latin and its learning among the clergy of his day Ælfred recommends its translation sometimes word for word, sometimes by sense. Interlinear and marginal glosses in medieval manuscripts had for centuries throughout Europe earlier conveyed both these cognitive conditions of the sense and accuracy of words or phrases but left the case unstated. At times the act of translation was disdained and disapproved of. A ninth-century Anglo-Saxon interlinear translation of the text of the elaborate and illuminated Lindisfarne Gospels is denigrated by a gloss as an act of educated vandalism defacing the veritable Word of God.

Medieval translation does embody further processes of conveyance. The edition of the poem (taken accurately from the original manuscript) observes standard palaeographical procedures. A glossary of dictionary definitions in modern English in its right-hand margin preserves the gap by a bridge between the 'interpretative translation' rendered in parallel on each facing-page; the bridge waxes and wanes within the modulation of the translation's recognition of the gorge in time, language, and culture between the medieval and the modern. The dictionary definitions of words are indicated by the abbreviation 'w' (word) and numerated according to their linear word order in the Anglo-Saxon text. This marginal glossing concentrates on the explanation of nouns and verbs. Definite/indefinite articles, pronouns and adverbs are in general more consonant and regular in Anglo-Saxon and can be referred to within the general glossary.

The runic ciphers of the Ruthwell Cross, which are ideographic, also require conveyance to the modern Roman alphabet; palaeographic procedures are relevant. Eroded/damaged runes are projected interpretations: (i) the partial reconstruction of runes are indicated by italicized Roman letters, and (ii) the total reconstruction of runes, where conservatively possible, are indicated by italicized Roman letters within square brackets. In panorama, the complete runic inscription has been presented in the visual order and sequence with which it borders the North (now East) and South (now West) sides of the Ruthwell Cross; these are read beginning from the top border on the left-hand corner (arrow 1), continuing to the right and vertically down the border (arrow 2). The inscription reading follows then from the top left-hand corner and vertically down the left-hand border (arrow 3).

The Dream of the Rood is a spiritual poem imbued with *godspel*, the words of the Gospel, the good news. Christianity is centrally concerned with the doctrine of salvation and how this is to be achieved; these redemptive sentiments are with which both art and literature will emanate and resonate. The drama of a moment, Christ *in extremis*, 'Christ was on Rood', appears stark and disparate in the translation due to the heightened significance of the event in Christian spirituality. Anglo-Saxon generic terms and details in the poem, however, portray a vernacular particularism in relation to religious terms. A central Christian term for 'Cross' is unmentioned in the *Dream of the Rood* but must be implicitly understood from the varied vocabulary of 'tree', 'beam/beacon', 'gallows', 'the best of woods', and 'rood' which represent it.

English words in general are commonly longer than their direct and recognized Anglo-Saxon antecedents. The original verbal inflection of this the earliest recorded period of the English language has been largely loosened and distended. The sphere of subject and predicate are now more extended and explored by modern pronouns and prepositions. In addition, the intensity, the intention, its subtlety and suppositions of any word such as 'wood' in Anglo-Saxon may now be largely lost with the prodigious linguistic shifts within the language. Yet a fidelity to reproduce this word simply even as it in orthography is, remarkably unchanged and intact, will with the translation refract at the very least where we cannot possibly reflect the sentiments of a society divided so by the ages.

The standard double-stressed syllabic half-lines of Anglo-Saxon in English poetry have long been ci-devant. The appliance of regular or modern metrical metre to the translation of medieval text rather than enhance may impede emphasis and effect within the original; the verse given here is free in form. Rhythm and line-length are determined by course and effluence within the medium of Modern English thought, form, and expression. The random and intermittent alliteration deliberated throughout the translation inculcates its pervasive order and presence in the original Anglo-Saxon text.

Debate about the non-use, use, and abuse of archaisms is itself old in argument. At times words such as 'thither' have been chosen to sound its hastily gathered assembly; 'thanes' and 'slayers' maintain an aura of Anglo-Saxon heroicism for Christ and the Cross of Victory. The word 'direly' has been adopted based on its Modern English definitions of the ominous and of dread that are synonymous with both scriptural and the poem's dark portentuous environ of the Crucifixional event; the Latinic derivatives of *dirus* also remain cogent. The synchronism of two or more meanings within one word was common to Anglo-Saxon and early Germanic languages (Old Icelandic, in particular); this is evident in *The Dream of the Rood*. In Anglo-Saxon this beam (of the Cross) is also a beacon. In the translation, as it is governed by fluvial rhythms and contexts contemporary and medieval, the expression 'beam and beacon' is represented in text as: (a) by both words conjoined by the conjunctive 'and', (b) by implied parallelism as 'the brightest of beams/All that beacon . . . ', (c) or by either word singularly stated to express a perceived emphasis. Another exemplar that occurs repeatedly in the text is 'sweat and blood'.

Translation is the art of exposition. Conceding that such should shy from and is ever inept in its accuracy, the interpretative translation can readily seek further afield in its relative understanding. By providing supplementary Cross-related texts, undirected by commentary, it is hoped that the reader may by their experience of *The Dream of the Rood* enhance appreciation and understanding. The Latin Cross texts have been chosen for their continued popularity, then and now, within the liturgy of Holy Week. The two Irish vernacular Cross poems have been added to indicate medieval distinctions between the significance of the sign of the Cross (Mugrón's Hymn) and the physical Cross (Blathmac Poem).

Plate I: East (now South) face of the cast of the Ruthwell Cross
in Durham Cathedral, Iconography & Inscriptions.

© Department of Archaeology, University of Durham. Photographer T. Middlemas.

Plate II: West (now North) face of the cast of the Ruthwell Cross
in Durham Cathedral, Iconography & Inscriptions.
© Department of Archaeology, University of Durham. Photographer T. Middlemas.

Plate III: North (now East) side of the Ruthwell Cross
in Dumfries, Scotland, Runic Phrasal Units I & II.
© Department of Archaeology, University of Durham. Photographer T. Middlemas.

Plate IV: South (now West) side of the Ruthwell Cross
in Dumfries, Scotland, Runic Phrasal Units III & IV.
© Department of Archaeology, University of Durham. Photographer T. Middlemas.

29

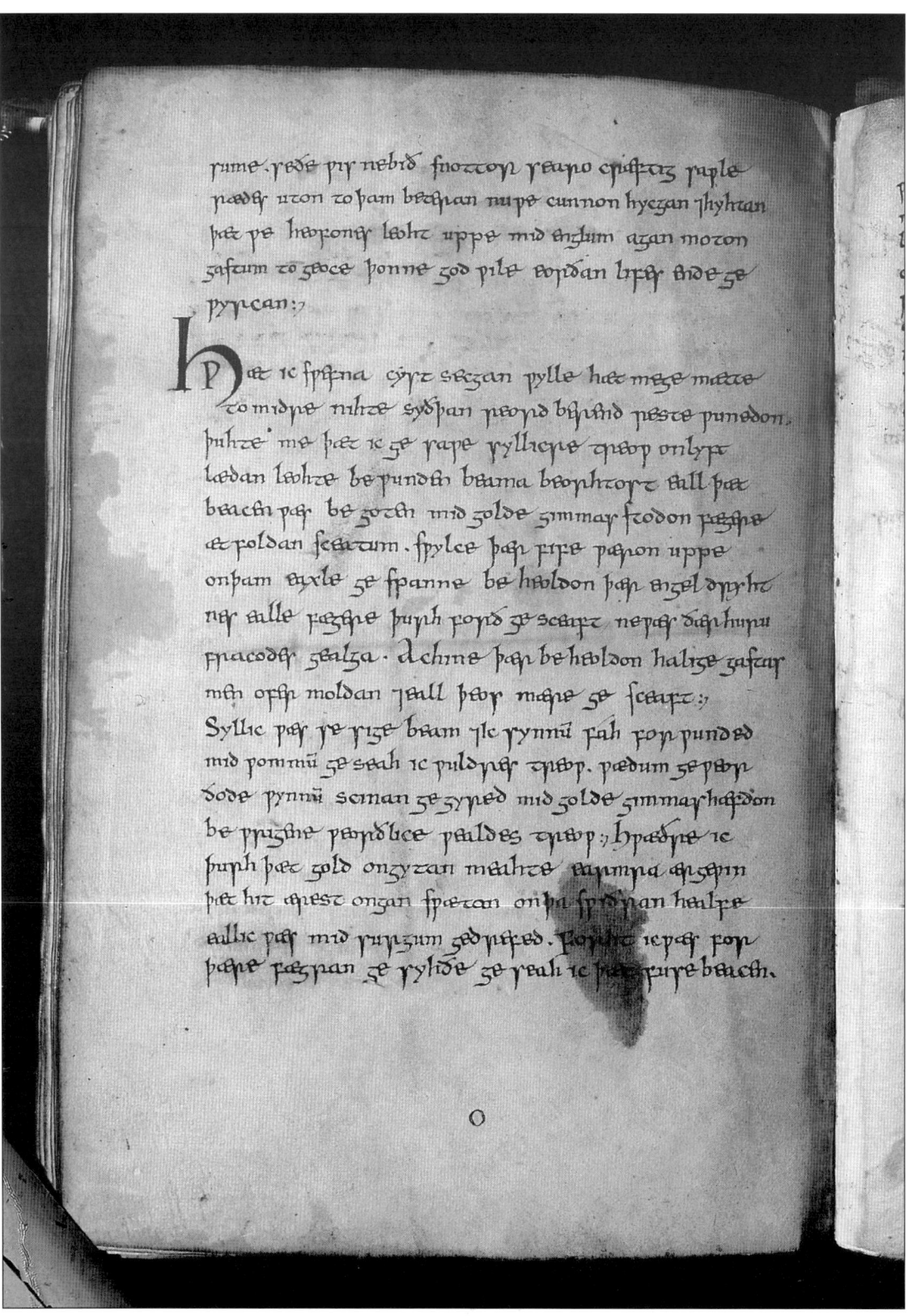

Plate V: The Vercelli Book, fol. 104v.

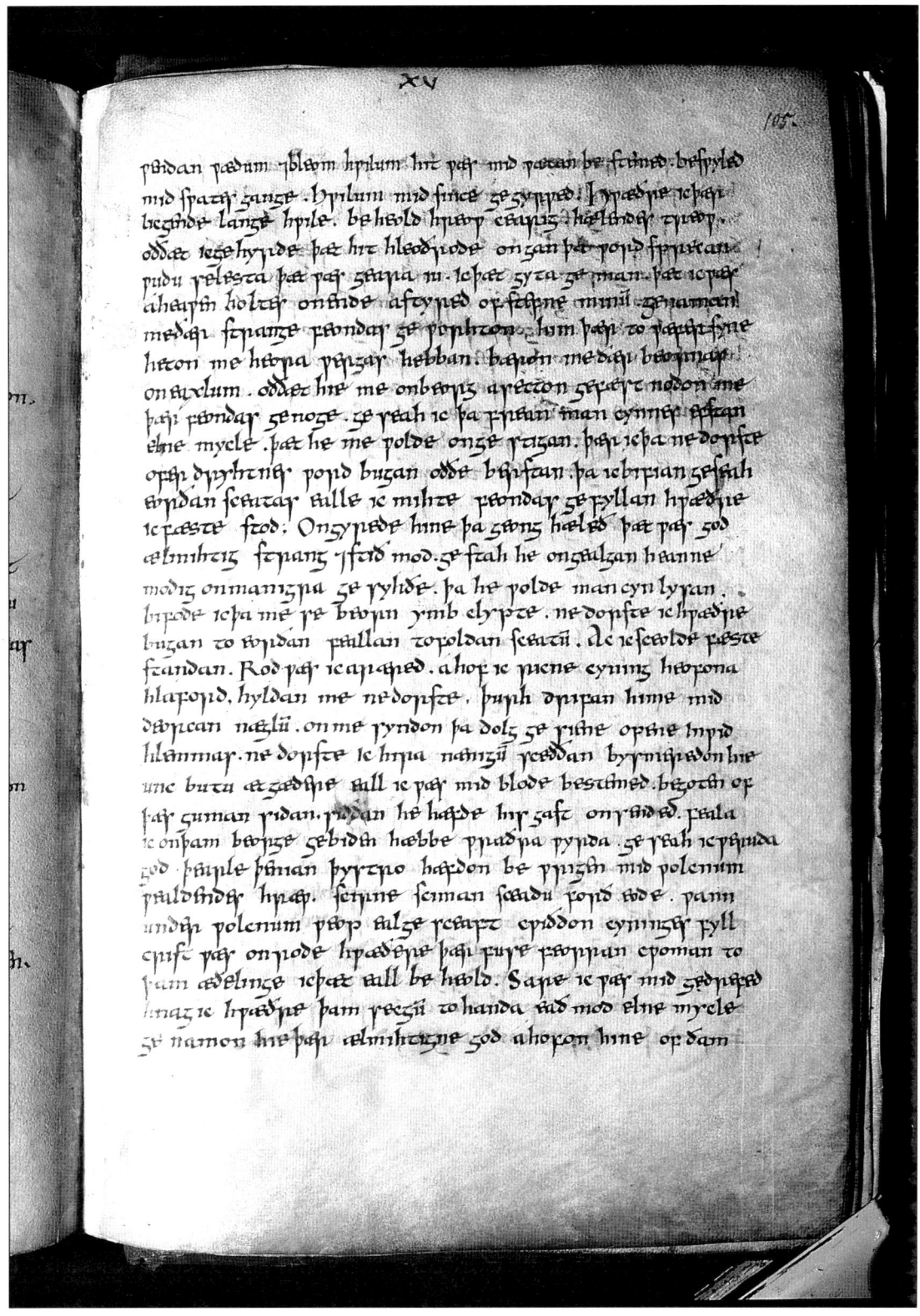

Plate VI: The Vercelli Book, fol. 105r.

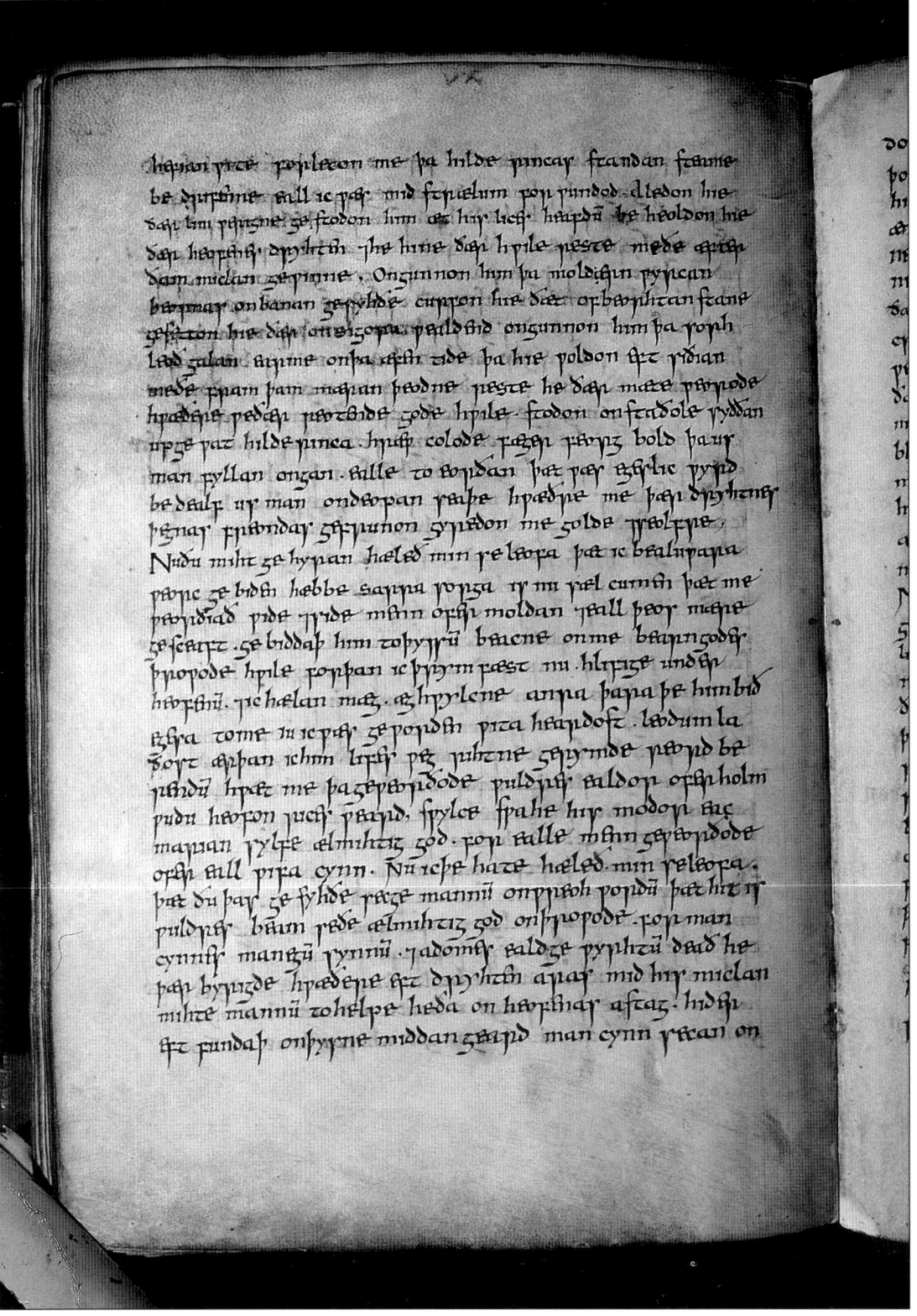

Plate VII: The Vercelli Book, fol. 105v.
© Capitolo Metropolitano di S. Eusebio, Vercelli.

32

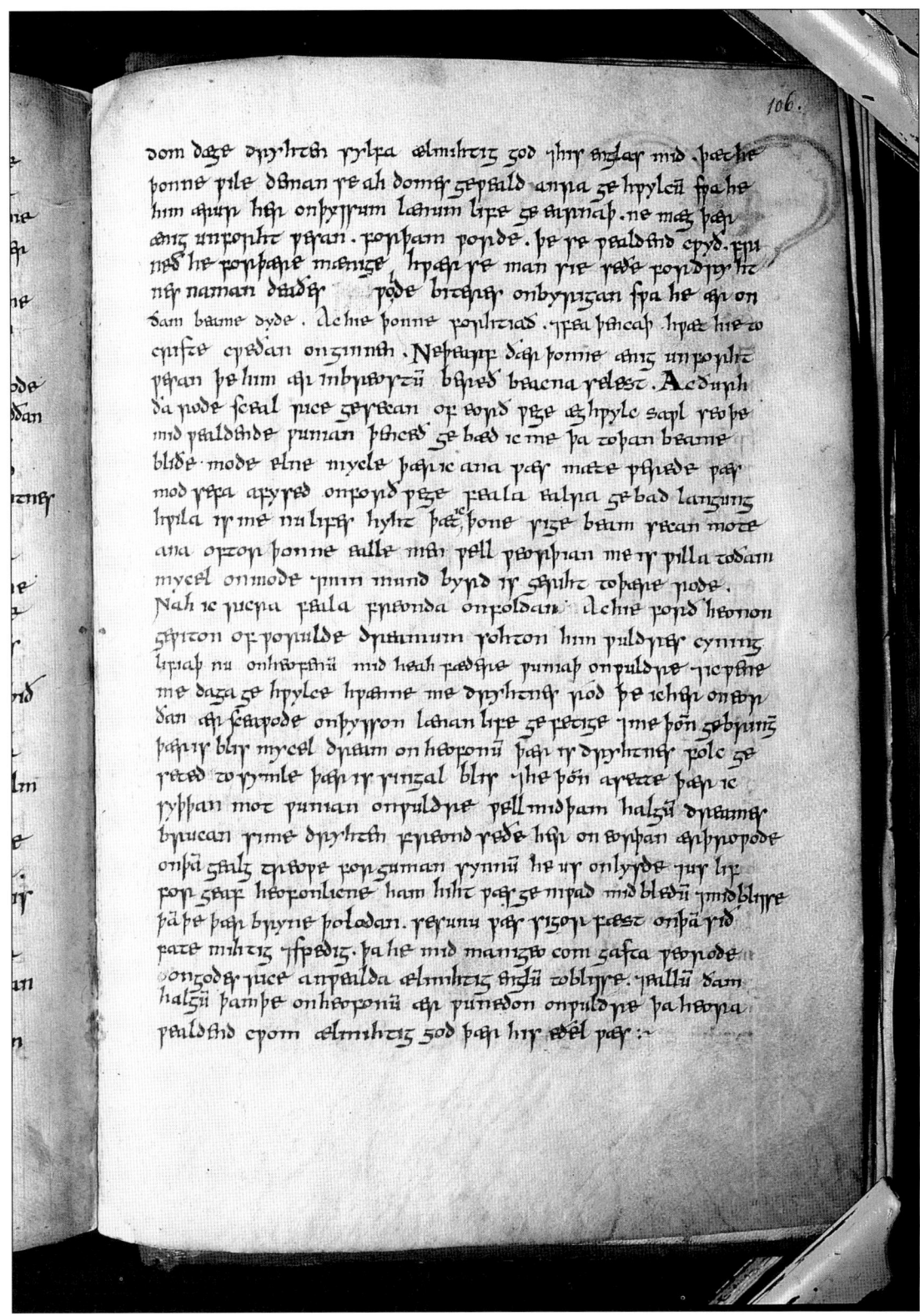

Plate VIII: The Vercelli Book, fol. 106r.

Plate IX: The Brussels Cross.

Ruthwell Runic
Poetic Text

READING AND EDITORIAL PROCEDURES OF THE RUNES

The terms left and right are designated as the relative position as seen by the observer of the cross. Both runic phrasal units I & III begin on the left-hand corner of the narrow sides of the Ruthwell Cross and follow arrow 2. Both units II & IV begin at the top of the left side-border and continue vertically downwards and follow arrow 3. Runic letters, recognized/complete, are re-presented by Roman letters. Eroded/damaged runes are projected interpretations: (i) the partial reconstruction of runes are indicated by italicized Roman letters, and (ii) the total reconstruction of runes, where conservatively possible, are indicated by italicized Roman letters within square brackets. Certain archaic spellings have been modernized in the editing of the four runic phrasal units (p. 38). The text, with minor mod-ifications, is after R.I. Page in Okasha (1971), pp.11-12, corrected from Howlett (1974a), and supplemented from Howlett (1976a); some modifications have been made, however, based on editorial procedures and an interpretation of the runes. A Modern English translation follows on the facing-page (p. 39).

Fig. 1: Ruthwell Runic Text

On the top border of the panel

[OND] GERE

On right vertical border of panel

2	D Æ
	H I
	N Æ
	G O
	D A
	L M
	E Yo
	T T I
	G Þ
	A H
	E W
	A L
	D E
	O N
	G A
	L G
	U G
	I S T
	I G A
	[M] O D
	I G F
	[O R E
	A L L Æ]
	M E N
	[B] U G
	[. . . .]

On left vertical border of panel

3	[A H
	O F]
	I K R
	I I K N
	Æ K U
	N I Ng
	K H Ea
	F U N
	Æ S H
	L A F
	A R D
	H Æ L
	D A I K
	N I D A
	R S T Æ
	B I S M
	Æ R Æ D
	U U Ng
	K E T
	M E N
	B A Æ T
	G A D
	[R E] I K
	[W Æ S]
	M I Þ B
	L O D Æ
	[B] I S T
	E M I
	[D] B I
	[. . . .]

36

On the top border of the panel

ᛏᚪᚱᛁᚻᛏᛈᚪᚻᛖᚾ 1 ⟶

[+] KRIST WÆS ON

On right vertical border of panel			On left vertical border of panel		
ᚱᚠ	**2** ↓	RO	ᛗᛁ	**3** ↓	M I
ᛗᛁ		DI	ᚦᛥ		Þ S
ᚻᚹ		HW	ᛏᚱᛖ		T R E
ᛖᚦ		EÞ	ᛚᚢ		L U
ᚱᚠ		RÆ	ᛗᚷ		M G
ᚦᛖ		ÞE	ᛁᚹ		I W
ᚱᚠ		RF	ᚢᚾ		U N
ᚢᛥᚠ		USÆ	ᛗᚠᛗ		D Æ D
ᚠᛏᚱ		F EaR	ᚠᛚᛖ		A L E
ᚱᚠᚾ		RAN	ᚷᚻᚢ		G D U
ᚪᚹᚠ		KWO	ᚾᚻᛁᚠ		N H I Æ
ᛗᚢᚠ		MUÆ	ᚻᛁᛏᚠ		H I N Æ
ᚦᚦᛁᛚ		ÞÞIL	ᛚᛁᛗᚹ		L I M W
ᚠᛏᛁᛚ		ÆTIL	ᛟᚱᛁᚷ		Œ R I G
ᚠᚾᚢ		ANU	ᚾᚠᚷᛁ		N Æ G I
ᛗᛁᛥ		MIK	ᛥᛏᚠ		S T O
ᚦᚠᛏᚠ		ÞÆTA	ᛗᛗᚢ		D D U
ᛚᛒᛁᚻ		LBI*H*	ᚾᚻᛁᛗ		*N* H I M
ᛏᛚᚻ		[*Ea*L D]	ᚠᛏᚻ		[Æ T *H*
ᛥᚱᛗ		SAR[*E*]	ᛁᛥᛚᛁ		I S] L I
ᛁᛥᚹᚠ		IKWÆ	ᛥᚠᛥ		K Æ S
ᛥᛗᛁᚦ		SMI[Þ]	ᚾᛏᚠ		[*H Ea*] F
ᛥᚠᚱ		SO*R*	ᛗᚢᛗ		[*D U*] M
ᚷᚢᛗ		GUM	ᛒᛁᚾᛏ		[*B I*] *H* Ea
ᚷᛁᛗ		GID	ᛚᛗᚢ		[*L*] *D* U
ᚱᛟᚠᛁ		R Œ [*F I*]	ᚾᚻᛁ		[*N*] *H* I
ᛗᚾᚾ		D H [*N*]	ᚠᚦᛖ		[Æ] Þ E
ᚠᚷᛁᚾ		A G [*I K*]	ᚱᚻᛏ		[*R H Ea*
		[. . . .]	ᚠᚢᚾ		*F U N*]
					[. . . .]

Runic Phrasal Unit I (North (now East) Side, Top & Right Border)

[+ *Ond*]geredæ Hinæ God Alme3ttig
þa He walde on galgu gistiga,
[*m*]oðig f[*ore allæ*] men.
[*B*]ug[*a ic ni dorstæ ac scealde fæstæ standa.*]

Runic Phrasal Unit II (North (now East) Side, Left Border)

[*Ahof*] ic riicnæ Kyningc,
Heafunæs Hlafard, *h*ælda ic ni dorstæ.
*B*ismæræðu ungket men ba ætgad[*re*]; ic [*wæs*] *m*iþ blodæ [*b*]istemi[*d*],
bi[*goten of þæs Guman sida siþþan He His gastæ sendæ.*]

Runic Phrasal Unit III (South (now West) Side, Top & Right Border)

[+] Krist wæs on rodi.
Hweþræ þer fusæ fearran kwomu
æþþilæ til anum: ic þæt al bi*h*[*eald*].
Sar[*æ*] ic wæs mi[*þ*] so*r*gum gidrœ[*fi*]d h[*n*]ag [*ic þam secgum til handa.*]

Runic Phrasal Unit IV (South (now West) Side, Left Border)

*Mi*þ stre*l*um giwundad
Alegdun hiæ *H*inæ limwœrignæ;
Gistoddu*n* him [*æt His*] *l*icæs [*hea*]f[*du*]m;
[*bi*]hea[*l*]du[*n*] *h*i[*æ*] þe[*r Heafunæs Dryctin; ond He Hinæ þer hwilæ restæ.*]

God Almighty stripped Himself
when He wished to mount the gallows,
brave in the sight of all men;
I dared not bow down, but had to stand fast.

I raised up a powerful King,
the Lord of Heaven; I dared not bow.
They reviled us both together.
I was drenched with blood shed from the man's side
after He had send forth His spirit.

Christ was on Rood.
Yet worthy ones gathered there eagerly from afar.
I beheld all that. Sorely was I with arrows afflicted.
I yielded unto the men, their hands.

Badly wounded by arrows, with His languid limbs
they laid Him down.
They stood by His body at the head.
They beheld there the Lord of the Heavens
and He rested Himself there for a while.

Plate X: East (now South) face of the Ruthwell Cross
in Dumfries Scotland, Iconography & Inscription.
© Department of Archaeology, University of Durham. Photographer T. Middlemas.

The Dream
of the Rood

Hwæt! Ic swefna cyst   secgan wylle   [f. 104v]   (w. 5 to tell; w. 6 wish or will)
h[w]æt me gemætte   to midre nihte,   (w. 3 dreamed)
syðþan reordberend   reste wunedon.   (w. 2 speech-bearer; w. 4 were)
     Þuhte me þæt ic gesawe   syllicre treow   (w. 6 wonderful)
on lyft lædan, leohte bewunden,   5   (w. 3 to be lifted up; w. 5 wrapped)
beama beorhtost.   Eall þæt beacen wæs   (w. 1 beam of wood or ray of light)
begoten mid golde;   gimmas stodon   (w. 1 sprinkled; w. 4 gems)
fægere æt foldan sceatum;   swylce þær fife   (w. 3 earth, ground; w. 4 corners)
          wæron
uppe on þam eaxlegespanne.   Beheoldon þær   (w. 4 cross-beam, junction of the cross)
          engel Dryhtnes ealle,   (w. 1 angel)
fægere þurh forðgesceaft.   Ne wæs ðær huru   10   (w. 3 creation)
          fracodes gealga.   (w. 1 of the wicked one; w. 2 gallows)
Ac hine þær beheoldon   halige gastas,   (w. 6 spirits)
men ofer moldan,   ond eall þeos mære gesceaft.   (w. 3 earth; w. 7 great, glorious)
     Syllic wæs se sigebeam   ond ic synnum fah,   (w. 4 victory-beam; w. 8 stained)
forwunded mid wommum.   Geseah ic wuldres   (w. 3 sins; w. 4 saw)
          treow,
wædum geweorðode   wynnum scinan,   15   (w. 1 clothing; w. 4 to shine)
gegyred mid golde;   gimmas hæfdon   (w. 1 adorned)
bewrigene weorðlice   weald[end]es treow.   (w. 1 clothed; w. 2 worthily)
Hwæðre ic þurh þæt gold   ongytan meahte   (w. 1 however; w. 6 to perceive)
earmra ærgewin,   þæt hit ærest ongan   (w. 1 of wretched; w. 2 former strife)
swætan on þa swiðran healfe. Eall ic wæs mid   20   (w. 1 to sweat; w. 4 on the right)
          sorgum gedrefed.   (w. 2 troubled)
Forht ic wæs for þære fægran gesyhðe.   Geseah   (w. 1 afraid; w. 7 vision, sight)
          ic þæt fuse beacen   (w. 3 eager)
wendan wædum ond bleom;   hwilum hit wæs   [f. 105r]   (w. 1 to change; w. 2 clothing)
          mid wætan bestemed,   (w. 3 made wet)
beswyled mid swates gange,   hwilum mid since   (w. 3 of blood; w. 4 flow; w. 7 treasure)
          gegyrwed.   (w. 1 adorned)
Hwæðre ic þær licgende   lange hwile   (w. 4 lying)
beheold hreowcearig   Hælendes treow,   25   (w. 2 sorrowful; w. 3 Saviour's)
oððæt ic gehyrde   þæt hit hleoðrode.   (w. 6 spoke)
Ongan þa word sprecan   wudu selesta: (w. 5 piece of wood; w. 6 good, great)
     'þæt wæs geara iu,   ic þæt gyta geman,   (w. 4 long ago; w. 8 may remember)
þæt ic wæs aheawen   holtes on ende,   (w. 4 cut down; w. 5 of the forest)
astyred of stefne minum.   Genaman me ðær   30   (w. 1 removed; w. 3 trunk, root)
          strange feondas,   (w. 2 enemies)
geworhton him þær to wæfersyne,   heton me   (w. 5 show, spectacle)
          heora wergas hebban.   (w. 2 outlaw, criminal)
Bæron me ðær beornas on eaxlum,   oððæt hie   (w. 4 men, warriors; w. 6 shoulders)
          me on beorg asetton,   (w. 3 mound, hill)
gefæstnodon me þær feondas genoge.   Geseah ic   (w. 1 fastened; w. 5 enough, many)
          þa Frean mancynnes   (w. 2 Lord; w. 3 of mankind)
efstan elne mycle   þæt he me wolde on gestigan.   (w. 1 to make haste)
Þær ic þa ne dorste   ofer Dryhtnes word   (w. 5 dared)
bugan oððe berstan,   þa ic bifian geseah   35   (w. 3 to burst, break; w. 6 to tremble)
eorðan sceatas.   Ealle ic mihte   (w. 2 corners)
feondas gefyllan,   hwæðre ic fæste stod.   (w. 2 to fell, strike down)
     Ongyrede hine þa geong hæleð,   þæt wæs God   (w. 1 stripped)

42

Listen! Let me tell you about the best of dreams,
what I dreamed about at around midnight,
after the bearers of voices took their rest.
It seemed to me that I saw a most wondrous tree raised aloft,
enveloped in light, the brightest of beams. *5*
All that beacon was encrusted with gold.
Gems stood out, beautiful at the earth's corners;
likewise there were five upon the shoulder-span.
All fair things throughout time and creation
beheld there the messenger of the Lord. *10*
Indeed, that was not a criminal's gallows,
but holy spirits and men throughout the earth
and all this glorious creation beheld it there.
Splendid was that victory-tree,
and I was stained with sins, terribly wounded by evildoing. *15*
I saw the tree of glory, honoured by its garments,
shining beautifully, clothed in gold;
gems had covered the Ruler's tree in splendour.
Yet through that gold I could perceive the ancient struggle of a wretched people,
in that it first began to sweat on the right side. *20*
I was completely overcome by sorrows;
frightened I was by that fair sight.
I saw that restless beam and beacon ever-changing its garments and colours;
at times it was made wet with moisture, drenched with the flow of blood and sweat,
at times adorned with treasure. *25*
Moreover, lying there for a long while,
I watched, troubled with sorrows, the Saviour's tree
until I heard its voice.
Then the best of woods began to speak in words:

'That was long ago. *30*
I still remember that I was hewn down at the edge of a forest,
cut off from my roots.
Strong enemies seized me there,
made a show and mockery of me for themselves,
ordered me to raise their condemned men aloft. *35*
Then men bore me on their shoulders
until they finally set me up on a hill.
Enemies enough fastened me there.
Then I saw the Lord of mankind hastening with great courage
in His urgent need to mount upon me. *40*
Then I dared not there against the Lord's word bend or break
when I saw that the corners of the earth did shake.
I could have felled all enemies but I stood fast.
Then the young warrior stripped himself,

ælemihtig,

strang ond stiðmod;   gestah he on gealgan
    heanne,   40   (w. 3 courageous; w. 7 gallows)
                                    (w. 1 high, lofty)
modig on manigra gesyhðe,   þa he wolde mancyn
    lysan.   (w. 4 sight, vision; w. 8 mankind)
                                      (w. 1 to redeem)
Bifode ic þa me se beorn ymbclypte;   ne dorste
    ic hwæðre bugan to eorðan,   (w. 1 trembled; w. 7 to embrace)
                                      (w. 3 to bow down)
feallan to foldan sceatum.   Ac ic sceolde fæste
    standan.   (w. 1 to fall)

Rod wæs ic aræred.   Ahof ic ricne Cyning,   (w. 1 rood; w. 4 raised up)
heofona Hlaford;   hyldan me ne dorste   45   (w. 1 of heaven)
Þurhdrifan hi me mid deorcan næglum;   on me   (w. 1 to pierce; w. 5 dark; w. 6 nails)
    syndon þa dolg gesiene,   (w. 3 wounds)
opene inwidhlemmas.   Ne dorste ic hira   (w. 2 malicious wounds)
    nænigum sceððan.   (w. 2 to harm, injure)
Bysmeredon hie unc butu ætgædere.   Eall ic   (w. 1 mocked, insulted; w. 4 both)
    wæs mid blode bestemed,   (w. 4 made wet)
begoten of þæs guman sidan,   siððan he hæfde   (w. 1 poured out; w. 4 man's)
    his gast onsended.   (w. 2 spirit; w. 3 sent forth)

    Feala ic on þam beorge gebiden hæbbe   50   (w. 5 hill, mound)
wraðra wryda.   Geseah ic weruda God   (w. 1 of cruel; w. 2 fates; w. 5 of hosts)
þearle þenian.   Þystro hæfdon   (w. 1 severely; w. 2 to stretched out)
bewrigen mid wolcnum Wealdendes hræw,   (w. 1 covered; w. 3 clouds; w. 5 corpse)
scirne sciman;   sceadu forð eode,   (w. 1 bright; w. 2 light; w. 3 shadow)
wann under wolcnum.   Weop eal gesceaft,   55   (w. 1 dark, black; w. 4 wept)
cwiðdon Cyninges fyll.   Crist wæs on rode.   (w. 1 lamented, mourned; w. 3 fall)
    Hwæðere þær fuse feorran cwoman   (w. 3 hastening; w. 4 from afar)
to þam æðelinge.   Ic þæt eall beheold.   (w. 3 Lord, Prince; w. 7 witnessed)
Sare ic wæs mid [*sorgum*] gedrefed,   hnag ic   (w. 1 deeply; w. 6 overcome; w. 7 bent)
    hwæðre þam secgum to handa,   (w. 3 men)
eaðmod elne mycle.   Genamon hie þær æleimihtigne 60 (w. 1 humble; w. 2 zeal; w. 4 seized)
    God,
ahofon hine of ðam hefian wite.   Forleton me   [f. 105v]   (w. 1 raised up; w. 5 grim; w. 6 torture)
    þa hilderincas   (w. 2 warrior)
standan steame bedrifenne;   eall ic wæs mid   (w. 3 covered, drenched)
    strælum forwundod.   (w. 1 arrows, darts)
Aledon hie ðær limwerigne,   gestodon him æt   (w. 1 laid down; w. 4 weary in limb)
    his lices heafdum;   (w. 3 head)
beheoldon hie ðær heofenes Dryhten,   ond he   (w. 4 heaven, sky)
    hine ðær hwile reste,   (w. 4 rested)
meðe æfter ðam miclan gewinne.   Ongunnon him   65   (w. 1 exhausted; w. 5 battle)
    þa moldern wyrcan   (w. 2 grave, tomb; w. 3 to make)
beornas on banan gesyhðe;   curfon hie ðæt of   (w. 1 men; w. 5 to cut out, carve)
    beorhtan stane,   (w. 1 bright, shining)
gesetton hie ðæron sigora Wealdend.   Ongunnon   (w. 4 of victories)
    him þa sorhleoð galan   (w. 3 lament, dirge; w. 4 to sing)
earme on þa æfentide;   þa hie woldon eft siðian   (w. 4 evening-time; w. 9 to depart)
meðe fram þam mæran þeodne;   reste he þær   (w. 4 great, glorious; w. 5 prince)
    mæte weorode.   (w. 1 small; w. 2 host, multitude)
    Hwæðere we ðær [*g*]reotende gode hwile   70   (w. 4 wept)
stodon on staðole,   syððan [*stefn*] up gewat   (w. 3 position, foundation; w. 5 voice)

who was God Almighty, strong and resolute.   *45*
He mounted the high gallows,
brave in the sight of many,
since He wished to set mankind free.
I trembled when the man embraced me,
yet I dared not bow to earth, fall to the land's spread,   *50*
but had to stand fast.
A rood, I was lifted up.
I raised aloft a powerful king, Lord of the Heavens;
I dared not bow down.
They pierced me through with dark nails;   *55*
on me the cleaving wounds can be seen, these open wounds of malice.
I dared not injure any of them;
they reviled the two of us together.
I was all drenched with the blood shed from the man's side
after He had sent forth His Spirit.   *60*
On that hill I had to endure many dreadful things;
I saw the God of hosts direly stretched out.
The darkness had covered with clouds the Body of the Ruler,
the Illuminating Light.
His shadow went forth, dark under clouds.   *65*
All creation wept, lamented the King's death.

Christ was on Rood.

Yet eager ones thither came from afar to the Prince.
I beheld all that.
I was completely overcome by grief, but humbly,   *70*
yet with great bravery, I submitted myself to the hands of these men.
They seized Almighty God there;
they raised Him up with such sore torment.
The warriors forsook me, standing drenched in sweltering sweat.
I was all wounded with arrows.   *75*
Then with His languid limbs they laid Him down;
they stood by His body at the head.
They beheld there the Lord of the Heavens
and He rested Himself for a while, worn after the great battle.
These men began making a cave in the earth for Him,   *80*
in the sight of His slayers.
They carved it of bright stone and set within it the Ruler's treasures.
Then they began at evening to sing a lament for Him who was forlorn.
Later, when spent, they motioned to take leave from the Glorious Prince;
He rested there with a bare gathering.   *85*
But we, weeping there for a long while, stood our ground
after the cry of the warriors went aloft.

hilderinca;   hræw colode,   (w. 1 of warriors; w. 2 corpse)
fæger feorgbold.   Þa us man fyllan ongan   (w. 1 fair, beautiful; w. 2 body)
ealle to eorðan;   þæt wæs egeslic wyrd!   (w. 6 fearful; w. 7 fate, event)
Bedealf us man on deopan seaþe.   Hwæðre me   75   (w. 1 buried; w. 6 pit)
        þær Dryhtnes þegnas,   (w. 3 thanes)
freondas gefrunon, ...   (w. 2 heard of)
gyredon me   golde ond seolfre.   (w. 1 adorned, dressed)
    Nu ðu miht gehyran,   hæleð min se leofa,   (w. 5 hero)
þæt ic bealuwara weorc   gebiden hæbbe,   (w 3 dwellers in evil, evil men)
sarra sorga.   Is nu sæl cumen   80   (w.1 of painful; w. 2 sorrows)
þæt me weorðiað   wide ond side   (w. 3 adore, honour)
menn ofer moldan   ond eall þeos mære gesceaft,   (w. 3 earth; w. 8 creation)
gebiddaþ him to þyssum beacne.   On me Bearn   (w. 5 symbol, sign, standard)
        Godes
þrowode hwile.   Forþan ic þrymfæst nu   (w. 1 suffered; w. 5 glorious)
hlifige under heofenum,   ond ic hælan mæg   85   (w. 1 rise, tower; w. 6 to heal, save)
æghwylcne anra   þara þe him bið egesa to me.   (w. 1 every; w. 2 of them; w. 7 awe)
Iu ic wæs geworden   wita heardost,   (w. 1 long ago; w. 4 become)
leodum laðost,   ærþan ic him lifes weg   (w. 2 hostile; w. 3 before)
rihtne gerymde,   reordberendum.   (w. 1 proper; w. 3 speech-bearer, man)
Hwæt, me þa geweorðode   wuldres Ealdor   90   (w. 4 honoured; w. 6 Prince, Lord)
ofer holmwudu,   heofonrices Weard,   (w. 2 wood on the hill; w. 3 heaven)
swylce swa he his modor eac,   Marian sylfe,   (w. 1 just as; w. 8 herself)
ælmihtig God,   for ealle menn
geweorðode   ofer eall wifa cynn.   (w. 4 & w. 5 womankind)
    Nu ic þe hate,   hæleð min se leofa,   95   (w. 4 command)
þæt ðu þas gesyhðe   secge mannum,   (w. 4 sight, vision)
onwreoh wordum   þæt hit is wuldres beam,   (w. 1 reveal; w. 7 beam of wood /light)
se ðe ælmihtig God   on þrowode   (w. 6 suffered)
for mancynnes   manegum synnum   (w. 2 mankind's)
ond Adomes   ealdgewyrhtum.   100   (w. 3 ancient or former deeds)
Deað he þær byrigde;   hwæðere eft Dryhten   (w. 4 tasted; w. 5 however)
        aras   (w. 1 arose)
mid his miclan mihte   mannum to helpe.   (w. 3 great; w. 4 power)
He ða on heofenas astag.   Hider eft fundaþ   (w. 5 ascended; w. 8 come)
on þysne middangeard   mancynn secan   (w. 3 middle earth; w. 5 may tell)
on domdæge Dryhten sylfa,   [f.106r] 105   (w. 2 Doomsday, Judgement Day)
ælmihtig God,   ond His englas mid,   (w. 5 angels)
þæt he þonne wile deman,   se ah domes geweald,   (w. 5 to judge; w. 7 may have)
anra gehwylcum   swa he him ærur her   (w. 2 everyone; w. 6 earlier)
on þyssum lænum   life geearnaþ.   (w. 3 fleeting, transitory)
Ne mæg þær ænig   unforht wesan   110   (w. 5 unafraid; w. 6 to be)
for þam worde   þe se Wealdend cwyð.   (w. 6 Saviour)
Frineð he for þære mænige   hwær se man sie,   (w. 1 will ask; w. 9 may be)
se ðe for Dryhtnes naman   deaðes wolde[1]   (w. 7 may intend)
biteres onbyrigan,   swa he ær on ðam beame   (w. 2 to taste)
        dyde.   (w. 1 did)
Ac hie þonne forhtiað,   ond fea þencaþ   115   (w. 4 will be afraid; w. 6 little)
hwæt hie to Criste   cweðan onginnen.   (w. 5 to say; w. 6 to begin)
Ne þearf ðær þonne ænig   *an*forht wesan   (w. 6 very frightened, terrified)
þe him ær in breostum bereð   beacna selest.   (w. 5 breast; w. 7 of signs; w. 8 best)

The body cooled, fair seat of the spirit.
Then we were all felled to the earth.
That was a terrifying event! 90
We were buried in a deep pit.
The Lord's thanes, His friends, heard;
they adorned me with gold and silver.
Now you can hear, my beloved warrior, how I,
the work of evil men, have endured painful sorrows. 95
Now the time has come for mankind to honour me far and wide;
men throughout the earth and all this glorious creation
pray for themselves to this beacon.
On me God's Son suffered for a while.
I, powerful now, because of that 100
tower aloft under the heavens,
and I can heal all who are in awe of me.
For many years I was seen as the cruellest of tortures,
most hateful to the people, before I prepared
the true way of life for them, the bearers of voices. 105
Behold, the Prince of Glory, the Guardian of the Heavenly Kingdom,
honoured me then above all the trees of the hill,
just as Almighty God highly honoured His mother, Mary herself,
above all the race of women for the sake of mankind.
Now I command that you, my beloved warrior, 110
announce this vision to men,
reveal in words that this is the beam of glory
which Almighty God suffered upon
for mankind's many sins and Adam's ancient deeds.
He tasted death there, 115
but the Lord rose again in His great power to help mankind.
He then ascended into the heavens.
He will come again onto this middle-earth
to seek out mankind on Doomsday.
The Lord Himself, Almighty God, together with His angels, 120
He who has power to give eternal glory,
according to the way each person has behaved
during his transient life on earth,
will come in order to give judgement.
Then no one can be without fear 125
because of the speech which the Ruler will make.
He will ask before the multitude of the dead
where the man is who for the Lord's name
was willing to taste bitter death,
as He once did on the beam. 130
But they will be full of fear,
and few will then know what they may begin to say to Christ.
But no one who has borne on his breast the best of beacons
need be too much afraid.

Ac ðurh ða rode sceal   rice gesecan   (w. 2 through; w. 4 cross)
of eorðwege   æghwylc sawl,   120   (w. 2 earth; w. 4 soul)
seo þe mid Wealdende   wunian þenceð.'   (w. 5 to dwell; w. 6 intends)
    Gebæd ic me þa to þan beame   bliðe mode,   (w. 1 prayed; w. 8 happy; w. 9 heart)
elne mycle,   þær ic ana wæs   (w. 5 alone)
mæte werede.   Wæs modsefa   (w. 1 small; w. 2 group; w. 4 mind)
afysed on forðwege;   feala ealra gebad   125   (w. 1 urged forth; w. 3 the departure)
langunghwila.   Is me nu lifes hyht   (w. 1 time of longing)
þæt ic[2] þone sigebeam   secan mote   (w. 4 wood of victory)
ana oftor   þonne ealle men,   (w. 2 often)
well weorþian.   Me is willa to ðam   (w. 2 to honour, adore)
mycel on mode,   ond min mundbyrd is   130   (w. 6 allegiance, protection)
geriht to þære rode.   Nah ic ricra feala   (w. 1 directed; w. 5 do not have)
freonda on foldan[3].   Ac hie forð heonon   (w. 1 friends; w. 3 earth; w. 7 hence)
gewiton of worulde dreamum,   sohton him   (w. 1 departed; w. 4 joys; w. 5 said)
        wuldres Cyning;   (w. 1 of glory; w. 2 King)
lifiaþ nu on heofenum   mid Heahfædere,   (w. 6 God the Father)
wuniaþ on wuldre.   Ond ic wene me   135   (w. 6 may hope, look for)
daga gehwylce   hwænne me Dryhtnes rod,   (w. 1 of days; w. 3 when)
þe ic her on eorðan   ær sceawode,   (w. 7 beheld)
on þysson lænan   life gefetige   (w. 3 transitory; w. 5 may fetch)
ond me þonne gebringe   þær is blis mycel,   (w. 4 may bring)
dream on heofonum,   þær is Dryhtnes folc   140   (w. 6 Lord's; w. 7 people)
geseted to symle,   þær is singal blis;   (w. 1 placed; w. 6 everlasting; w.7 joy)
ond *me* þonne asette   þær ic syþþan mot   (w. 4 may be positioned; w. 8 may be)
wunian on wuldre,   well mid þam halgum   (w. 4 fully)
dreames brucan.   Si me Dryhten freond,   (w. 1 joys; w. 2 to enjoy, partake of)
se ðe her on eorþan   ær þrowode   145   (w. 6 previously; w. 7 suffered)
on þam gealgtreowe   for guman synnum.   (w. 3 gallows-tree; w. 5 mankind)
He us onlysde   ond us lif forgeaf,   (w. 3 redeemed; w. 7 gave, granted)
heofonlicne ham.   Hiht wæs geniwad   (w. 1 heavenly; w. 3 hope)
mid bledum ond mid blisse   þam þe þær bryne   (w. 2 glories; w. 9 burning hell-fire)
        þolodan.   (w. 1 suffered)
Se Sunu wæs sigorfæst   on þam siðfate,   150   (w. 4 victorious; w. 7 expedition)
mihtig ond spedig,   þa he mid manigeo com,   (w. 7 multitude)
gasta weorode,   on[4] Godes rice,   (w. 1 souls)
Anwealda ælmihtig,   englum to blisse   (w. 1 Sovereign Lord)
ond eallum ðam halgum   þam þe on heofonum   (w. 4 holy ones)
        ær
wunedon on wuldre,   þa heora Wealdend cwom,   155   (w. 1 dwelt; w. 3 glory)
ælmihtig God,   þær his eðel wæs.   (w. 5 homeland)

Through the Rood every soul who with the Ruler wishes to dwell   *135*
must seek out the Kingdom, away from the way of the world.'

I prayed then to that beam content of spirit,
with great valour, there where I was alone with a handful of followers.
My heart was made restless for the way forth;
I underwent many hours of longing.   *140*
It is now the joy of my life that I,
being more frequently alone than other men,
may seek out that victory-tree and honour it fully.
Determination for this is great in my mind,
and my hope for protection is completely in the Rood.   *145*
I do not have many powerful friends on earth;
they passed forth earlier from the joys of the world,
found their way to the King of Glory.
They live now in heaven with the Father on high
and dwell in glory;   *150*
I hope too every day for the time when the Lord's Rood,
which I here on earth have already looked upon,
will from this fleeting life fetch me,
and bring me to where there is great happiness in heaven,
where the people of the Lord are seated at the feast,   *155*
where joy is never-ending.
I trust that He will sit me down
where I may from then on dwell in glory,
and enjoy eternal bliss consummate with the saints.
May the Lord be a friend to me,   *160*
Who here on earth once suffered on the gallows-tree for the sins of men.
He set us free and gave us everlasting life, a heavenly home.
For those who endured the burning of hell
hope was renewed with rejoicing and exultation.
The Son was victorious on that journey,   *165*
mighty and successful when He came with a multitude,
a company of souls, into God's Kingdom.
The Sovereign Lord Almighty,
to the delight of the angels and all those sanctified
who had in heaven till this dwelt in glory,   *170*
then He their Ruler came; Almighty God,
there His homeland was.

Textual Notes:

The Anglo-Saxon text is accompanied by a select glossary in the right-hand column, which provides a rendering into Modern English of words that may be unfamiliar, primarily verbs, nouns, adjectives, and adverbs. Each corresponds with the letter 'w' and by number to the word order within the line. Both line numberings of the poem in the original text and in the translation are collated independently, being indicated respectively by normal and italic script. The folio number, abbreviated as [f.], is also cited to indicate the location of the poem within the Vercelli Codex.

L.2, w.1	h[*w*]æt] *MS.* hæt.
L.17, w.3	weald[*end*]es] *MS.* wealdes.
L.20, w.1	s*o*rgum] *MS.* surgum.
L.59, w.5	[*sorgum*] supplied from the Ruthwell text.
L.65, w.2	mold*e*rn] *MS.* moldærn: the MS reading has dots over and under the *a* of *æ*, which usually indicates the omission of such a letter.
L.70, w.4	[*g*]reotende] *MS.* reotende.
L.71, w.5	[*stefn*] supplied by Kluge.
L.113, w.7	[1]wolde]: emmended by Swanton from 'þrowolde'; 'pro' erased and 'l' interlined.
L.117, w.6	*a*nforth] *MS.* unforth.
L.127, w.2	[2]ic]: interlined.
L.132, w.3	[3]on]: erased after foldan.
L.142, w.2	*m*e] *MS.* he.
L.152, w.3	[4]o]: erased before on.

The Dream of the Rood has attracted and given cause to a century of linguistic debate and interpretation; for its scholarship see Swanton (1987; repr. 1992), pp. 103-39.

Brussels Cross Inscription & Dedication

Plate XI: The Brussels Cross Inscription.

Poetic Inscription

Rod is min nama. Geo ic ricne cyning
bær byfigynde, blode bestemed.

Prose Dedication

Þas rode het Æþlmær wyrican ond Aðelwold hys beroþo[r]
Criste to lofe for Ælfrices saule hyra beroþor.

Rood is my name. Trembling once, I bore
a powerful king, made wet with blood.

Æthlmær and Athelwold, his brother, ordered this rood to be made so as to praise Christ for the soul of Ælfric, their brother.

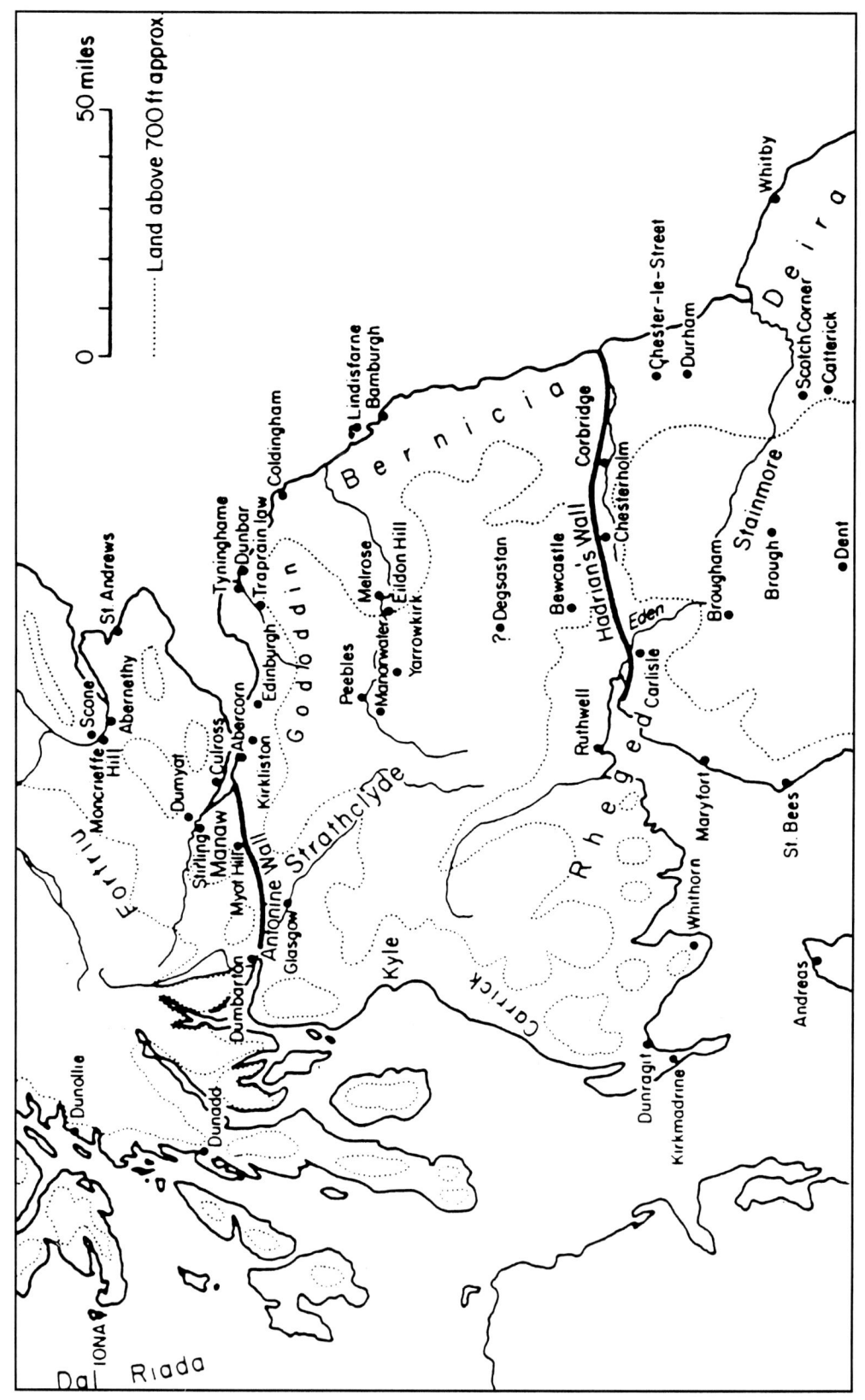

Fig 2: Map of southern Scotland and northern England.
© A.P. Smith, Edward Arnold Ltd., and Edinburgh University Press.

Contemporary Latin & Vernacular Cross Hymns & Poems

No language in Christendom was uttered in isolation; the Christianity of the Anglo-Saxon was imbibed with the learning of Latin while the Anglo-Saxon language was bordered with the languages of Scotland, Wales, and Ireland. This series of contemporary Latin and vernacular Cross hymns and poems complement the Old English texts. They not only indicate a broader religious context but also a shared tradition. *Vexilla Regis Prodeunt* and *Pange Lingua* by Fortunatus and *Victimae Paschali Laudes* by Wipo were sung in the liturgy of Lent and Holy Week in the Medieval Church. The Latin texts continue to be used in the liturgy of Lent and Holy Week. The Mugrón and Blathmac extracts from the Irish tradition are meditative pieces on the role of the Cross as protector and in the history of salvation; both themes are emphasized in *The Dream of the Rood*.

Vexilla Regis Prodeunt

Venantius Fortunatus (*circa* AD 530 – ?609) was born in northern Italy. He became chaplain to the community of nuns founded by Radegund at Poitiers in western France a few years previously. Formerly, she had been the wife of the Merovingian King, Chlotar I. Fortunatus wrote a number of light verse epistles to the saint and her friend, Agnes, who was the superior of the community, and some magnificent hymns. *Vexilla Regis Prodeunt*, in Ambrosian stanzas (i.e. the simple, popular metre used by St. Ambrose of Milan (*circa* AD 340-97) for hymns), was composed by Fortunatus to celebrate St. Radegund's reception of a relic of the True Cross from the Emperor of Constantinople. This hymn was usually sung during the Lenten liturgy, at Vespers on Passion Sunday (the Sunday before Palm Sunday).

Vexilla regis prodeunt,
Fulget crucis mysterium,
Quo carne carnis conditor
Suspensus est patibulo.

The banners of the king onward proceed,
the mystery of the Cross shines forth,
where in the Flesh, who made our flesh,
was hung on the gallows.

Confixa clavis viscera,
Tendens manus, vestigia,
Redemptionis gratia
Hic immolata est hostia.

His body pierced by nails,
stretching forth His hands and feet,
for the sake of our redemption
here He was sacrificed as Victim.

Quo vulneratus insuper
Mucrone dirae lanceae,
Ut nos lavaret crimine,
Manavit unda, sanguine.

Whereon while He hung, His sacred side
was transfixed by a soldier's spear;
to cleanse us of our guilt He shed forth
water mingled with His blood.

Impleta sunt quae concinit
David fideli carmine,
Dicendo nationibus:
'Regnavit a ligno Deus'.

Fulfilled is what David
foretelling sang in true song,
when he declared onto the nations:
'God has reigned from a tree's wood.'

Arbor decora et fulgida,
Ornata regis purpura,
Electa digno stipite
Tam sancta membra tangere.

O becoming and illuminate tree,
adorned with the regent's purple,
chosen, with its worthy bole,
to touch such holy limbs.

Beata, cujus bracchiis
Pretium pependit saeculi!
Statera facta est corporis
Praedam tulitque tartari

Be you blessed, on whose branches
hung the world's recompense.
A scales was made of His body, from
which is taken away the condemned to hell.

Fundis aroma cortice,
Vincis sapore nectare,
Iocunda fructu fertili
Plaudis triumpho nobili.

You pour forth aroma from the bark,
you exceed nectar in savour.
Rejoicing in your lush fruit
you applaud in glorious triumph.

Salve ara, salve victima
De passionis gloria,
Qua vita mortem pertulit
Et morte vitam reddidit.

Hail altar, hail Victim,
from the glory of the Passion,
with which life endured death
and by death rendered forth life.

Pange Lingua

This hymn is also written by Venantius Fortunatus, and for the same occasion for which he wrote *Vexilla Regis Prodeunt*. It is composed in a similar metre to that of the hymn *Corde Natus* by Prudentius (AD 343 – *circa* AD 410). Alike to *Vexilla Regis Prodeunt* it is replete with the wordplay of which Fortunatus is renowned. This hymn was sung on Good Friday, during the ceremony of the Veneration of the Cross.

Pange, lingua, gloriosi proelium certaminis
Et super crucis tropaeo dic triumphum nobilem,
Qualiter redemptor orbis immolatus vicerit.

De parentis protoplasti fraude factor condolens,
Quando pomi noxialis morte morsu corruit,
Ipse lignum tunc notavit, damna ligni ut solveret.

Hoc opus nostrae salutis ordo depoposcerat,
Multiformis perditoris arte ut artem falleret
Et medellam ferret unde, hostis unde laeserat.

Quando venit ergo sacri plenitudo temporis,
Missus est ab arce patris natus, orbis conditor,
Atque ventre virginali carne factus prodiit.

Vagit infans inter arta conditus praesepia,
Membra pannis involuta virgo mater adligat,
Et pedes manusque, crura stricta pingit fascia.

Lustra sex qui jam peracta tempus implens corporis,
Se volente, natus ad hoc, passioni deditus,
Agnus in crucis levatur immolandus stripite.

Hic acetum, fel, arundo, sputa, clavi, lancea;
Mite corpus perforatur; sanguis, unda profluit,
Terra, pontus, astra, mundus quo lavantur flumine.

Crux fidelis, inter omnes arbor una nobilis,
Nulla talem silva profert flore, fronde, germine;
Dulce lignum dulce clavo dulce pondus sustinens.

Flecte ramos, arbor alta, tensa laxa viscera,
Et rigor lentescat ille quem dedit nativitas,
Ut superni membra regis mite tendas stipite.

Sola digna tu fuisti ferre pretium saeculi,
Atque portum praeparare nauta mundo naufrago,
Quem sacer cruor perunxit fusus agni corpore.

Sing, O tongue, of the strife in the glorious battle
and tell of the noble triumph won upon the trophy of
the Cross; how the Redeemer of the world was
sacrificed and was victorious.

The Creator, grieving the perfidy of our first-formed
parent, when by eating of the ominous apple, he fell
down onto death; then He marked Himself out with the
wood of a tree, to undo the damning by the wood of a tree.

The work of our salvation was the order ordained,
that He by art might outwit the art of the variform
deceiver, and seek healing from the very source
where the foe had worked his harm.

When therefore the fullness of the holy time came,
sent from His Father's citadel He was born, the Creator
of the world, and, clad in flesh, He came forth from the
Virgin's womb.

The infant cries, hemmed in a cramped manger.
His Virgin Mother, wrapping in swaddling clothes,
binds His limbs; His hands and feet she arrays
puttees in tight bands.

When thirty years were now accomplished and having
completed His earthly life, of His own free will, and born
for this purpose, given up to His Passion, the Lamb is
raised up on the trunk of the Cross to be sacrificed.

Then the vinegar, the gall, the reed, the spitting,
the nails, and the spear; His tender body is pierced, and
blood and water flow. Earth, sea, sky, and the
the world are cleansed in its flood.

Faithful Cross, the one noble tree among all,
no forests bear your scion in flower, leaf, or fruit;
O sweet wood, O sweet nails suspending,
sustaining.

Bend your boughs, O lofty tree, relax your too rigid
sinews, and let the rigour relent which birth has
bestowed you, so that your bole may gently
support the limbs of the heavenly King.

You alone are worthy to bear the world's recompense,
and like a ship to provision the shipwrecked world
for port, which the sacred blood has anointed,
poured forth from the body of the Lamb.

Victimae Paschali Laudes

Wipo (d. AD 1050) was a priest from Burgundy (or possibly from Swabia in southern Germany). He was a chaplain to Emperor Conrad II, whose reign he chronicled. He is considered to be the author of the words and music of this fine Easter poetic sequence, *Victimae Paschali Laudes,* which is still recited in the Easter Liturgy today. A poetic sequence is a hymn-like text, often in rhythmical prose, sung after the epistle at mass on certain important liturgical feasts. Wipo's sequence was sung on Easter Sunday and on the following Sundays of the Easter season. It is composed in rhythmical prose with each strophe and consecutive anti-strophe containing the same number of syllables (i.e. stanza 2 has the same number of syllables as stanza 3; 4 as 5; and 6 as 7). The first half of the sequence is in varied assonance, the remainder in double rhyme.

Victimae paschali laudes
Immolent Christiani.

To the paschal Victim, let Christians
give praise.

Agnus redemit oves;
Christus innocens patri
Reconciliavit
Peccatores.

The Lamb has redeemed the sheep;
and Christ, the Sinless One,
has to the Father sinners
reconciled.

Mors et vita duello
Conflixere mirando;
Dux vitae mortuus
Regnat vivus.

Death and Life
in a wondrous conflict strove;
the Prince of Life, once dead,
now lives and reigns.

'Dic nobis Maria
Quid vidisti in via?'
'Sepulchrum Christi viventis
Et gloriam vidi resurgentis.

'Tell us, O Mary,
what did you see on the way?'
'The tomb of the living Christ,
I saw, and the glory of the Resurrected.

Angelicos testes,
Sudarium et vestes.
Surrexit Christus spes mea,
Praecedet suos in Galilaea.'

Angelic testimonies,
the napkin and the garments;
Christ, my hope, has risen;
He goes before His own into Galilee.'

Credendum est magis soli
Mariae veraci
Quam Judaeorum turbae fallaci.

One should solely believe in
veracious Mary,
rather than in the beguiling mob of Jews.

Scimus Christum surrexisse
A mortuis vere;
Tu nobis, victor rex, miserere.

We know that Christ has truly risen
from the dead:
On us, O Victor, O King, have mercy.

Mugrón (extract)

This Irish poem is annotated to both Colum Cille (d. AD 597) and his much later successor Mugrón (AD 965–81). Linguistically the poem is of the tenth or eleventh century; it is probable that Mugrón has dedicated this verse to his founding saint, Colum Cille. The poem has twelve quatrains, the metre maintaining a regular syllabic sextet for each line. The Cross is invoked, petitioned repeatedly for protection against the forces of evil. Common to Irish, Welsh, and Icelandic traditions, the poem is a charm known as a *Lorica*, which recalls St. Paul's scriptural exhortation to wear spiritual armour in the battle against evil (Eph 6:14-18), (Thess 5:8), and (cf. Is 59:17). The text and translation follows Murphy (1956; repr. 1998) with some minor modifications to the translation.

Cros Chríst tarsin ngnúisse,		Christ's Cross over this face,
tarsin gclúais fon cóirse.		and thus over my ear.
Cros Chríst tarsin súilse.		Christ's Cross over this eye.
Cros Chríst tarsin sróinse.		Christ's Cross over this nose.
Cros Chríst tarsin mbélsa.	5	Christ's Cross over this mouth.
Cros Chríst tarsin cráessa.		Christ's Cross over this throat.
Cros Chríst tarsin cúlsa.		Christ's Cross over the back of this head.
Cros Chríst tarsin táebsa.		Christ's Cross over this side.
Cros Chríst tarsin mbroinnse		Christ's Cross over this belly
(is amlaid as chuimse).	10	(so it is fitting).
Cros Chríst tarsin tairrse.		Christ's Cross over this lower belly.
Cros Chríst tarsin ndruimse.		Christ's Cross over this back.
Cros Chríst tar mo láma		Christ's Cross over my arms
óm gúaillib com basa.		from my shoulders to my hands.
Cros Chríst tar mo lesa.	15	Christ's Cross over my thighs.
Cros Chríst tar mo chasa.		Christ's Cross over my legs.
Cros Chríst lem ar m'agaid.		Christ's Cross to accompany me before me.
Cros Chríst lem im degaid.		Christ's Cross to accompany me behind me.
Cros Chríst fri cach ndoraid		Christ's Cross to meet every difficulty
eitir fán is telaig.	20	both on hollow and on hill.
Cros Chríst sair frim einech		Christ's Cross eastwards facing me.
Cros Chríst síar fri fuined.		Christ's Cross back towards the sunset.
Tes, túaid cen nach n-anad,		In the North, in the South unceasingly
cros Chríst cen nach fuirech.		may Christ's Cross straightway be.
Cros Chríst tar mo déta	30	Christ's Cross over my teeth
nám-tháir bét ná bine.		lest injury or harm come to me.
Cros Chríst tar mo gaile.		Christ's Cross over my stomach.
Cros Chríst tar mo chride.		Christ's Cross over my heart.
Cros Chríst súas fri fithnim.		Christ's Cross up to broad heaven.
Cros Chríst sís fri talmain.	35	Christ's Cross down to earth.
Ní thí olc ná urbaid		Let no evil or hurt come
dom chorp ná dom anmain.		to my body or my soul.

60

The Poems of Blathmac (extract)

The Irish poem *Tair cucom, a Maire boíd* is devoted to the Virgin Mary and Christ, her Son. It is ascribed to Blathmac whose father Cú Brettan, a royal retainer, is mentioned in the saga of the Battle of Allen (AD 718); sagas are often historically unreliable, however. The poem contains 149 stanzas. J. Carney assigns the early date of *circa* AD 750-70 to its composition but it is plausibly later. The text and translation follows Carney (1964; repr. 1989) with some minor modifications to the translation.

Ó du-ruidmiset am-ne Ísu combu thorise do-luid Longinus iar sin diä guin cosind láigin.	220	When they thought thus that Jesus could be approached, Longinus then came to slay him with the spear.
Ó fu-rócbath a chride, mac ríg na secht noebnime, do-rórtad fín fu roenu, fuil Críst triä geltoebu.		The King of the seven holy heavens, when his heart was pierced, wine was spilled upon the pathways, the blood of Christ flowing through his gleaming sides.
Toesca toebraith coimdeth dil ro-bathais mullach nÁdaim, dég ad-rumedair int eú cruchae Críst ina béulu.	225	The flowing blood from the body of the dear Lord baptized the head of Adam, for the shaft of the Cross of Christ had aimed at his mouth.
Dond fuil chétnai – ba cain n-am! – is trait ron-ícc in n-ógdall, ossé díb dornnaib co glé oc imbeirt inna láigne.	230	By the same blood (it was a fair occasion!) quickly did he cure the fully blind man who, openly with two hands, was plying the lance.
Láthirsit dó dig séto ar laindi a mochéco; con-mescat – gním nádbu chet! – domblas dó ar fínacet.	235	They presented him with a parting drink through eagerness for his speedy death; they mix (illicit deed!) gall for him with vinegar.
Ar-rócaib guth cain cathach oc atuch a noebathar: 'Cair rom-léicis, a Dé bí, dom daíri, dom dochraiti?'	240	He raises a beautiful protesting voice beseeching his holy Father: 'Why have you abandoned me, living God, to servitude and distress?'
To-celt grian a soillsi sain, ro-coíni a flaithemain, luid diantemel tar nem nglas, búiristir rian trethanbras.		The sun hid its own light; it mourned its lord; a sudden darkness went over the blue heavens, the wild and furious sea roared.
Ba dorchae uile in bith, talam fu durbae rochrith; oc Ísu uasail aidid ro-memdatar márailich.	245	The whole world was dark; the land lay under gloomy trembling; at the death of noble Jesus great rocks burst asunder.

Fig. 3: The Scriptorium or Monastic Writing Room.
Book satchels hang overhead. (Drawing by David Rooney).
© The O'Brien Press, Dublin.

Representations & Forms of the Cross

This series of plates represent the wider scope and range of the Cross tradition throughout Europe in the early Middle Ages. Cross representations in the Lindisfarne Gospels and the Book of Kells, silver- and gold-plated processional and pectoral crosses, and the free-standing crosses of Ireland and Scotland give witness to the prevalence of Cross art and to a tradition shared with the Ruthwell Cross, *The Dream of the Rood*, and the Brussels Cross. A brief description of each plate is provided in pp. 79-80.

Plate XII: St. Martin's Cross, West face.

Plate XIII: Apse Mosaic, S. Apollinare in Classe, Ravenna.
© Scala Museum, Florence.

Plate XIV: Gold Pectoral Cross (Egypt?).
© Byzantine Collection, Dumbarton Oaks, Washington, DC.

Plate XV: St. Cuthbert's Pectoral Cross.
© Dean & Chapter Durham Cathedral.

67

Plate XVI: Bewcastle Shaft, West face.
© Department of Archaeology, University of Durham. Photographer T. Middlemas.

Plate XVII: Ahenny North Cross, East face.
© Dúchas, The Heritage Service, Dublin.

69

Plate XVIII: The Cross Page (fol. 26v), the Lindisfarne Gospels.

© The British Library, London.

Plate XIX: *Chi-Rho* **Page** *(Christi autem generatio)* **(fol. 34r), the Book of Kells.**
© The Board of Trustees, Trinity College Library, Dublin.

71

Plate XX: Cross of Scriptures, Clonmacnoise, East face.
© Dúchas, The Heritage Service, Dublin.

Plate XXIa: Silver Processional Cross, Church of S. Maria in Valle.
© Museo Archeologico Nazionale, Cividale.

Plate XXIb: Silver Processional Cross, Church of S. Maria in Valle.
© Museo Archeologico Nazionale, Cividale.

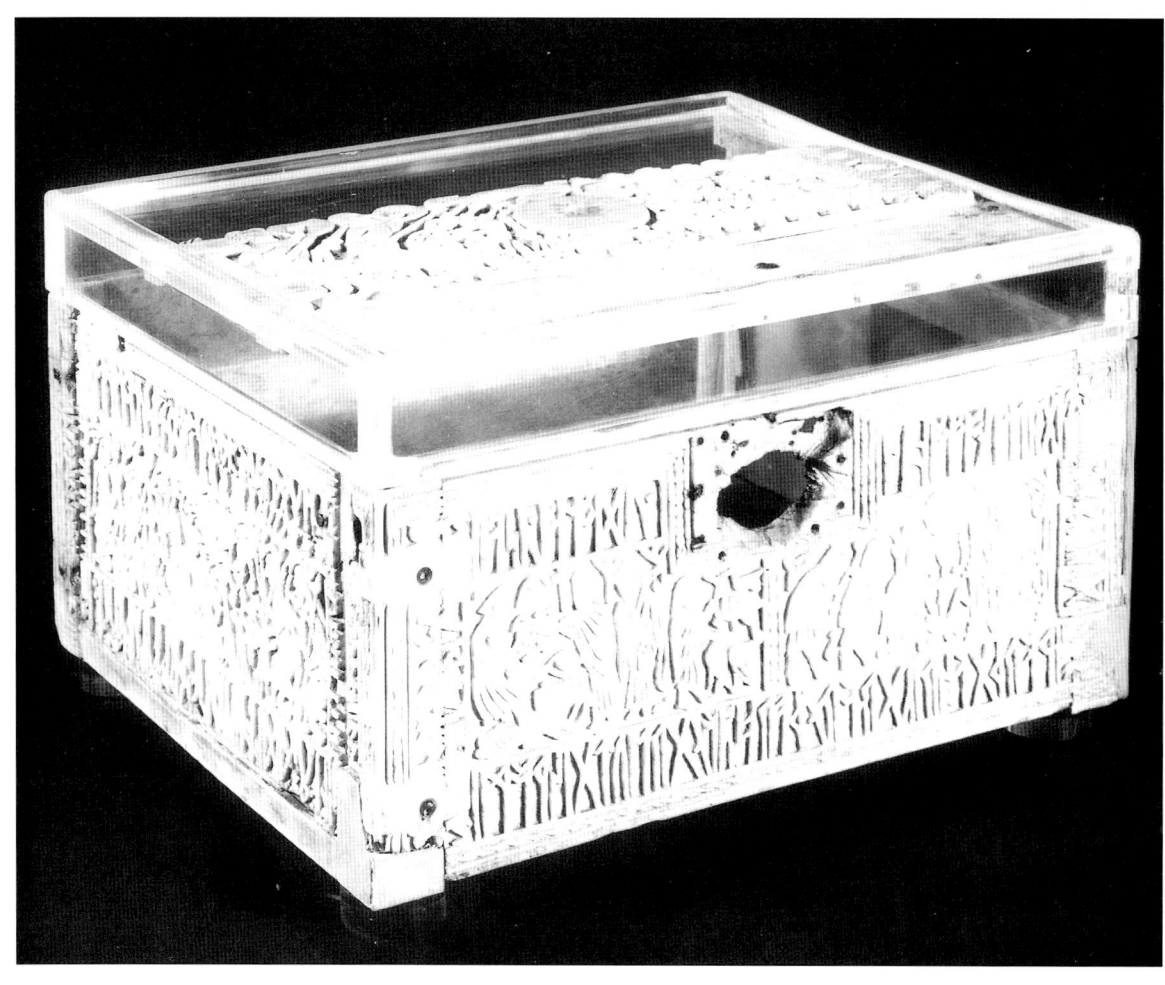

Plate XXII: Franks Casket.
© The British Museum, London.

Plate XXIII: Rupertus Cross.
© Dommuseum zu Salzburg.

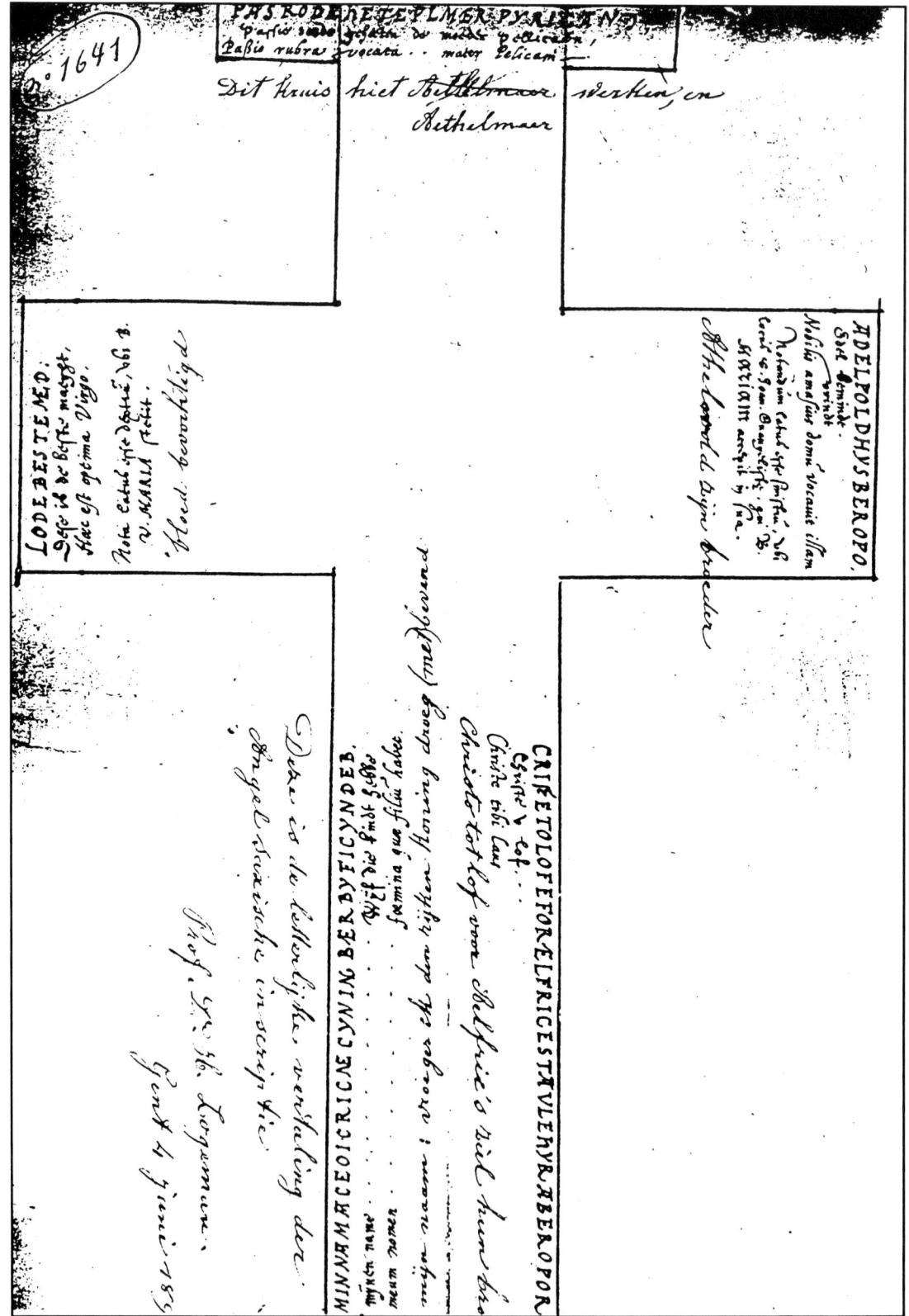

Fig. 4: Brussels Cross diagram, comprising of the cross inscription and a Latin translation from *circa* 1650, and a Dutch translation by Prof. H. Logeman dated 1894.

inscriptio est caracteribus et idiomate Anglo-Saxo-
nicis exarata, atque ita, ut censeo legenda:

+ Rodis minna mage oic riche cuning bær busigunde
blode bestemed; thas rode het Æthelmær wurican, and
Athelwoldhus berothor, Criste to lofe, for
Alfrices sawle, hira berothor.

Pars prior hujusce inscriptionis mihi obscura est.
Rodis, significat crucis.
minna, = amor
mage, = potens
oic =
riche, = fortis, potens, dives, in casu obliquo.
cyning bær, = rex, tulit, obtulit, &c.
busigynde, = trepidans; mutiens.
blode, = sanguinis.
bestemed, = cruentatus, a, um.
Sed nullum inde sensum sanum huc-usque conficere
satis. Cetera clara sunt, et Belgice sonant ita.
Dat (het) h'ruys heette Æthelmaer werken, mater
ende Athelwoldus broeder, tot lof van Christus
voor Alfrites zielen, haren (hunne) broeder.
                    et Latine:
Hanc crucem jussit Æthelmærus officii, ende Athel
woldus frater, ad laudem Christi, pro Alfrici
animas, sui fratris. —

Plate XXIV: Cross of Cong.
© The National Museum of Ireland, Dublin.

Plate Descriptions

Plate XII St. Martin's Cross, West face

St. Martin's Cross is situated west of the abbey on the island of Iona in western Scotland. It has been dated to the middle or second half of the eighth century. Unlike the nearby crosses of St. John and St. Matthew, the St. Martin Cross remains intact in its original base. The west face depicts iconographic scenes that include Daniel in the Lion's Den, the Sacrifice of Isaac and at its centre the Virgin and Child. Its east face is decorated with both serpent-and-boss and spiral ornament.

Plate XIII The Apse Mosaic, S. Apollinare in Classe, Ravenna

The city of Ravenna in north-eastern Italy was a prominent and prosperous Byzantine enclave in the fifth/sixth centuries. St. Apollinaris, the first bishop of Ravenna, was the local saint to whom this magnificent basilica was dedicated. The mosaic decoration is confined to the apse and so-called 'triumphal arch'. It is a composite work completed over several periods. In the semi-dome four bishops are situated between the lower windows flanked by angels in the arches. A roundel of Christ at the top is flanked by the symbols of the Four Evangelists with which following sheep from Bethlehem and Jerusalem emerge. The central jewelled cross is flanked by Moses and Elijah emerging from the clouds, watched by three sheep from below; this may represent the Transfiguration. The lower central figure represents a shepherd/priestly Apollinaris.

Plate XIV Byzantine Gold Pectoral Cross

The pectoral cross, a small portable cross (usually metallic), was worn by clerical orders of the priesthood around the neck during liturgical and devotional services. This gold pectoral cross originated in Egypt of the sixth or most probably the early seventh century. The Coptic art of Egypt was directly influenced at this period by the imperial artistic designs of Constantinople; the pectoral cross bears similarities to the cross of Justin II of Constantinople. The figures on the arms of the cross include the Virgin at the top, John the Baptist below, and two evangelists (right and left). The cross is now to be found among the Byzantine and Early Medieval Antiquities of the Dumbarton Oaks Collection, Washington DC, USA. Dimensions: height (8cm); width (5.3cm).

Plate XV St. Cuthbert's Pectoral Cross

St. Cuthbert (d. AD 687), abbot and bishop of Lindisfarne, is still today one of the most revered saints in the north of England. This seventh-century pectoral cross was found in St. Cuthbert's coffin in Durham. After the Viking assault on Lindisfarne in AD 875, the saint's body was eventually brought to Durham in AD 995. The cross is set with 12 garnets in each arm and the centre is roofed in gold setting containing another garnet under which there was probably a tiny relic. It is now in the care of the Dean and Chapter of Durham Cathedral. Dimensions: across (6.4cm).

Plate XVI The Bewcastle Shaft, West face

The Bewcastle Shaft was erected some years earlier than the Ruthwell Cross to which it is closely related; its cross-head is now missing. The east face depicts a continuous inhabited vine-scroll similar to that on the Ruthwell Cross. The south face displays vegetative scroll, a sundial and ornamentative interlace. On the west face two iconographic panels contained by arches are represented. The lower panel depicts a large bird perched on a man's arm (possibly St. John and the Eagle) as he directs a staff diagonally down towards a T-shaped object. A lengthy commemorative runic inscription, now damaged, is inscribed above; it begins with the sign of the cross and the term *þis sigbecn* ('this victory beam') and ends with the words *gebidaþ þaer sawle* ('pray for the soul'). The upper panel represents Christ in Judgement over the Beasts as on the Ruthwell Cross.

Plate XVII The Ahenny North Cross, East face

The Ahenny North Cross, Co. Tipperary, in southern Ireland is a fine early example of the Irish Celtic ringed cross. Unlike Anglo-Saxon stone crosses it is donned by a capstone. The beehive-shaped capstone is enigmatic but most probably symbolically signifies the basilica/dome of the church. Its decorative interlace is intricate and determinably linked to eighth/ninth century insular metalwork. On the four sides of its wide block base shallow carved iconography portrays an enigmatic funeral procession with horse and beheaded corpse, seven clerics, chariots and horses, and a menagerie of animals and activity. Dimensions: height (2.64m); shaft width (49cm).

Plate XVIII The Cross Page (fol.26v), the Lindisfarne Gospels

The Lindisfarne Gospels is an illuminated Latin Gospel Book, similar to the Book of Kells, dating from *circa* AD 698. Its provenance is early Northumbria in northern England, and it was commissioned in honour of St. Cuthbert, the famous bishop of Lindisfarne, who died in AD 687. A note in Anglo-Saxon inserted in the manuscript *circa* AD 950 – 970 by a priest called Aldred informs us of the origin of the manuscript. Aldred was responsible for the interlinear Old English word-for-word translation or gloss in the spaces between the lines of the Latin text. The Gospel Book remained at Lindisfarne until AD 875, when it accompanied the monks in their flight from invading Danes. From AD 883 – 995 the Lindisfarne community remained at Chester-le-Street, near Durham, finally settling at Durham itself in AD 995. The manuscript most likely lost its original binding during the period of the Dissolution of the Monasteries in the 16th century that was instigated by King Henry VIII. Early in the 17th century Sir Robert Cotton acquired it from Robert Bowyer, Clerk of the Parliaments, and today it remains in the safe keeping of the British Library in London, Catalogue No. Cotton Nero D. IV.

Plate XVIX Chi-Rho Page, (fol. 34r), the Book of Kells

The ninth-century illuminated Celtic Gospels, the Book of Kells, was considered by the twelfth-century Norman commentator, Giraldus Cambrensis, as 'the work of angels'. Its intricate decorative spiral and interlace defies the naked eye. Its provenance is disputed. It was most likely completed at either Iona in western Scotland or Ireland, with possible Pictish influences. The book was probably designated for the reading of important lections and/or display on the consecrated altar during primary liturgical seasons. Folio 34r, depicts the large ornate P of the *chi-rho* monogram. This begins the words *Christi autem generatio* (Mt 1:18) which initiates St. Matthew's account of the nativity.

Plate XX The Cross of Scriptures, Clonmacnoise, East face

This *circa* early tenth-century sandstone Celtic ringed High Cross stands to the west of the doorway of the Cathedral at Clonmacnoise. Clonmacnoise was an important and central early monastic site situated on the eastern banks of the River Shannon in the Irish Midlands. Like the Ruthwell Cross it is covered in iconographic panels. The interpretations of most of the panels are still a matter of conjecture. The base depicts quadrupeds and fabulous animals, chariots and horsemen, figures bearing croziers, and a damaged inscription in Irish. As is common on Irish High Crosses a house-shaped shrine dons the top of the cross. The ring centre depicts a Crucifixion scene and a Last Judgement scene on the west and east faces respectively. Dimensions: height: (3.15m); width (54cm).

Plate XXIa & Plate XXIb Silver Processional Cross, Cividale

The Cividale Processional Cross comes from S. Maria in Valle in northern Italy. It is now found in the Museo Archeologico Nazionale di Cividale. It dates from the second half of the eighth century. The cross is made from a single piece of wood and laminated in silver. It forms an equal-armed Latin cross with a cruciate figure of Christ in its ringed centre. Several inscriptions are inscribed on the cross in Latin: Over the head of Christ: *IHS NAZAREN*; Over the figure of the sun: *SOL*; Under the arms of Christ: (*M)ARIA ECE FILIVS TVOS - A DISCIPVLE ECCE MAT.* Dimensions: height (1.18m); width (86cm).

Plate XXII The Franks Casket

The Franks Casket (*circa* AD 730) is carved of whalebone and originates from the north of England. The casket now damaged is preserved in the British Museum; the right-hand side is in Florence. The panels portray diverse episodes and incidents from classical, Germanic, Judaic and Christian traditions. Foliage, scrolls, and interlace are woven in between. Three surrounding inscriptions are carved runes in Old English; a further fourth is in Latin of mixed runes and insular script. A description of the panels is as follows: Left-hand side: the finding of the twins, Romulus and Remus the founders of Rome, by four shepherds. The Lid: Egil the Archer, from the Norse saga, defends his homestead from armed attackers and archers. Front panel, Left side: an episode from the Germanic tale of Weland the Smith; Right side: the Adoration of the Magi with the three kings bearing gifts to the Virgin and Child. Rear panel: the triumphal sacking and entry of Emperor Titus into Jerusalem in AD 70. Right-hand side: an unknown Germanic legend. Dimensions: (22.9cm X 18.9cm X 12.9cm).

Plate XXIII The Rupertus Cross

Art historians date the Rupertus Cross roughly between AD 700-750. Tradition associates the cross with St. Rupertus, who founded the cathedral at Salzburg (circa AD 730); the cathedral, however, was not consecrated and the relics of St. Rupertus translated there until AD 774. Recently, its complex and profuse inhabited vine-scrolls have been compared to Northumbrian and Mercian sculpture; its animal-like volutes on the shaft are a *leitmotif* of Anglo-Saxon decorative style in the eighth century. The acanthus fronds on the cross arms parallel the renascent classical forms of the early Carolingian period; to surmise, Anglo-Saxon craftsmen may have been commissioned on the continent. Repoussé and chased with copper gilding, only 9 of 38 of its glass insets now exist. Dimensions: height (1.58m); width (94cm).

Plate XXIV The Cross of Cong

The High King of Ireland, Turlough O'Connor, had it commissioned and a relic of the True Cross enshrined within. It is dated by its inscriptions to *circa* AD 1125, and dedicated to the Bishop of Connaught, Domnall MacFlannacan U Dubthaig. Formed of oak, covered with plates of copper, it is decorated in the spiralling and intricate Norwegian Urnes style which was popular in Insular art at this period. A central boss is surmounted in convex crystal. The thirteen gem stones remaining of eighteen are regularly interspaced on the surrounding edges; the shaft terminates in the head of an animal connected to an ornamented sphere and the socket into which the shaft for carrying the cross in procession was inserted. Dimensions: length of shaft (76.2cm); span of arms (48.3cm); width of shaft/arms (2cm).

Background to Anglo-Saxon History & Language

A Brief Historical Outline of Anglo-Saxon England

Recent archaeological evidence has confirmed that the Anglo-Saxon occupation of Britain commenced fifty or so years before the traditionally accepted date of AD 449 recorded in the *Anglo-Saxon Chronicle*. The Angles, Saxons, and Jutes (as they were known) initially came at the request of Britons to provide protection against Celtic and Roman adversaries; ironically, they eventually gained control of a major part of the country. This did not culminate in the swift submission of the whole island under one Germanic king. In fact, the fortune of the Britons under the leadership of Mons Badonicus (AD 490-517) changed for the better, and they gained control of part of the western and south-midland regions that had been previously overrun by these Anglo-Saxon invaders.[1]

The arrival of Ireland's St. Columba in western Scotland in AD 565 proved to be a significant event because from this region – especially the island of Iona – Bishop Aidan and his followers brought Celtic Christianity to northern England. This is where the Christian faith began to flourish in England. Roman Christianity was introduced with the arrival of St. Augustine, who was dispatched at the request of Pope Gregory the Great to Canterbury in AD 595.[2] The Church Synod of Whitby in AD 664 addressed the variance between the Celtic and Roman Christian traditions, in particular the controversy over the dating of Easter, and concluded by promulgating the precedence of the Roman tradition throughout Anglo-Saxon England.[3]

The Anglo-Saxons settled in independent regions throughout the island. There were, for example, ten such territories south of the River Humber in AD 600. These communities were relatively isolated from each other by geographical boundaries such as mountains and rivers, and by hostile inhabitants. The social segregation of isolated communities usually led to pronunciation shifts within the shared lingua franca, developing certain distinctive dialectic features. What were originally individual or tribal characteristics would likely have been subsumed within larger flourishing communities; by AD 700 (the date of the earliest linguistic records for Old English) four distinct dialects could be identified: Northumbrian, Mercian, Kentish, and West Saxon.

Fighting and conflict between the vying kingdoms was common: one after the other they were temporarily subjugated under some powerful warrior-king. However, for a period of about one hundred years from the mid-seventh century the northern Anglo-Saxon kingdom of Northumbria enjoyed a period of comparative peace. Famous scholars such as Bede and Alcuin, the stone sculpture of the Bewcastle and Ruthwell Crosses, and the magnificent illuminated Gospel-book, the Lindisfarne Gospels, all emanated from this region. Despite this cultural and intellectual flowering, just four Anglo-Saxon kingdoms remained by AD 800: Northumbria, Mercia, Wessex, and East Anglia.

The first Scandinavian invaders came from Norway.[4] They landed at Portland, Dorset in AD 787, killing the reeve of Dorchester. They sailed on around the north of Scotland and set up communities in the Shetland and Orkney Islands and the Hebrides, as well as on the east coast of Ireland from where, in the tenth century, they proceeded to invade the west coast of England.

The Danes were also the instigators of a series of swift summer raids, hurriedly taking their plunder off back home with them. These did not abate until AD 851. After that year they are recorded in the *Anglo-Saxon Chronicle* as wintering on the Isle of Thanet. Over the next number of years there was intense hostile activity. One by one, the kingdoms of Northumbria, East Anglia, and Mercia ceased to exist as independent entities. In AD 878 Wessex too was nearly overturned, save for the skill

---

[1] A standard book on the history of Anglo-Saxon England is Stenton (1971; repr. 1989). Other important works are Campbell (1982; repr. 1991), Fisher (1992), Hill (1981), Hunter Blair (1962; repr. 1977), Jones (1976), Knowles (1963), Laing & Laing (1979), Marsh (1987), Oman (1993), Palgrave (1989), Southern (1953; repr. 1959), Webster & Blackhouse (1991), Whitelock (1974; repr.1979), Whittock (1986), Wilson (1981), and Wood (1987).

[2] The coming of Christianity to Anglo-Saxon England is well documented in Mayr-Harting (1991). See also *The Anglo-Saxon Chronicle* entries for AD. 596-784 in Garmonsway (1953; repr. 1972).

[3] On the Church Synod of Whitby, see Bede's *Ecclesiastical History of the English People*, Bk. III, Chapters xxv-xxvii, in Colgrave & Mynors (1969; repr. 1992). Other useful works to consult are Whitelock (1974; repr. 1979), and Hunter Blair (1970; repr. 1990).

[4] On the history of the Vikings, see Jones (1968; repr. 1990), & Loyn (1977).

of the famous Anglo-Saxon King Ælfred. His power and influence on the Wessex throne was affirmed after his successful military victory against the Danes at Ebbsfeet in that same year. His understanding of the principles of warfare revealed by his numerous campaigns against the Danes, and relayed in the *Anglo-Saxon Chronicle* (which he is purported to have commissioned) helped to regain military confidence among his people. This in conjunction with his promotion of culture, education, learning, and administration over the next twenty years until his death in AD 899 restored an immense sense of societal identity to the English. Ælfred more than any other Anglo-Saxon king realized that the strength of a society must be based on cultural as well as military prowess.[5]

By AD 880 Wessex was the only one of the four Anglo-Saxon kingdoms surviving. In the years following the Danes gained a permanent foothold in England and the boundaries of their kingdom, the Danelaw, were established. Another powerful army from France invaded in AD 892 resulting in more intense fighting and allies from Northumbria and East Anglia rallied to assist them. Wessex under King Ælfred and his successors won back territory from the settled Danes, coercing them to comply with English rule. By AD 954 the Scandinavian kingdom of York ceased to exist and the unification of England as one kingdom was realized. Consequently, Anglo-Saxon England, especially Wessex, enjoyed a period of comparative peace in the second part of the tenth century, similar to Northumbria in halcyon days a hundred years or so earlier.

Social and cultural stability, however transient, spurred the revival of Benedictine monasticism, which was instigated by Dunstan, Archbishop of Canterbury (AD 960-988). Scriptoria and manuscript production began to flourish. The four principal extant manuscripts containing the greater corpus of Old English poetry were compiled around the same time. These are the *Beowulf* codex (BL MS Cotton Vitellius A.XV), the Exeter Book (MS 3501 in the Library of the Dean and Chapter of Exeter Cathedral), the Junius MS (Bodl. Junius 11), and the Vercelli Book (Vercelli, Biblioteca Capitolare, CXVII) which contains the text of *The Dream of the Rood*.[6] In a short passage from *The Battle of Maldon* (ll. 50-4) one may even perceive what might be considered the beginnings of a sense of patriotism:

> Sege þinum leodum   miccle laþre spell,
> þæt her stynt unforcuð   eorl mid his werode
> þe will gealgean   eþel þysne,
> Æþelredes eard,   ealdres mines
> folc and foldan.[7]

> [Make known to your people a much more ominous tale,
> that here stands fearless an earl with his army
> who will safeguard this land,
> Æthelred's kingdom, my lord's
> own people and land.

Nevertheless, the statutes of King Canute officially acknowledging a threefold territorial division into Wessex, Mercia, and Danelaw still echo the partitions of an earlier era.[8] A volatile demographic reality in the tenth century may have provided the Anglo-Saxons with an awareness to record in writing their literature and learning for the prosperity of future generations to come. In the wake of the Norman Conquest of AD 1066, which marked the era of French rule throughout Anglo-Saxon England, this proved to be providential.

---

[5] On the reign of King Ælfred, see Asser's Life of King Ælfred in Keynes & Lapidge (1983), and *The Anglo-Saxon Chronicle* entries for AD 871-900 in Garmonsway (1953; repr. 1972). For standard histories on Ælfred the Great, refer to Frantzen (1986), & Williams (1951).

[6] Facsimiles of these manuscripts are in Malone (1963) (*Beowulf*); Chambers, Flower, & Förster (1933) (Exeter Book); Gollancz (1927) Junius 11; Sisam (1976) (Vercelli Book).

[7] *The Battle of Maldon* is edited in Scragg & Deegan (1991). This edition has a full *apparatus criticus* and provides detailed information on the historical background to the battle

[8] On King Canute (Knut), see Jones (1968; repr. 1990, esp. pp. 182-240, & Williams (1938).

The subsequent history of Anglo-Saxon England is well documented. The reigns of the Danish Æthelred 'the Unready' and Edward the Confessor were to be soon pressed upon by Harold's victory at Stamford Bridge near York and his defeat at Hastings in AD 1066.[9] A general historical overview of the entire period is outlined in Table 2 (pp. 92-3).

With rapid and continual social change the fortunes of Christianity fluctuated throughout the Anglo-Saxon period. The implications are crucial in order to critically comprehend the historical context of the poetic texts which are the focus of this book. The Christianity of the Roman Church was not readily accepted by the non-Christian Germanic invaders, who brought with them to England their own specific heroic code, a sophisticated social code and way of life. Despite the early Celtic Columban evangelization in the North, the teachings of St. Augustine and his followers at Canterbury, the standards of Romanization at the Synod of Whitby, etc., paganism still maintained a presence. A heathen called Penda, King of Mercia, for instance, murdered King Edwin of Northumbria in AD 632. Throughout the Anglo-Saxon period Christians inveighed against paganism. In a letter dated AD 797 condemning the recitation of pagan poetry to monks, Alcuin posed the now well-known question, 'What did Ingeld do with Christ?' Invading Danes brought their own form of Christianity with them. Both King Ælfred and King Ethelred acted as sponsors at the baptisms of foes. In AD 1012, during the lifetime of the two most famous Anglo-Saxon homilists, Ælfric and Wulfstan,[10] drunken Danes murdered Ælfeah, the Archbishop of Canterbury.

It is probable that the Christian poet composing in Old English between AD 680-850, when most of the present extant poetry was orally formulated, would have been a convert from paganism or the direct descendant of a converted pagan. If neither, he was part of a society where the struggle between the pagan Germanic religions and Christianity had not yet been resolved. Cædmon, who is reputed to be the first English poet, known to us, effectively brought together Christian subject-matter with Old English poetic style in a unique blend of Christian symbolism and Germanic heroic elements.[11] Christian poetry in Old English after Cædmon continued to adapt Germanic cultural features, as is the case with several stylistic and thematic features of *The Dream of the Rood*.

This crucial ambivalence is clearly seen in the Sutton Hoo ship burial site, which is both a memorial to the pagan King Rædwald (d. AD 624) and to the brevity with which he remained a Christian.[12] This site, located in East Anglia, was first excavated by archaeologists in 1939 just before the outbreak of World War II. It provides one of the most apt symbolic insights into the history of the period: a blend of the non-Christian and the Christian.

---

[9] See Kirby (1992), Whitlock (1977), and *The Anglo-Saxon Chronicle* entries for AD 910-1066 in Garmonsway (1953; repr. 1972).

[10] For samples of their works, see Swanton (1975; repr. 1993), pp. 136-201.

[11] On Cædmon, see Dobbie (1942), pp. xciv, clxx, 105, 198, and Smith (1933; repr. 1968). See also the account of the poet Cædmon in Bk IV, Chapter xxiv, of Bede's *Ecclesiastical History of the English* in Colgrave & Mynors (1969; repr. 1992).

[12] On Sutton Hoo, see Bruce-Mitford (1968; repr. 1972), (1975), (1978), & (1983), and Evans (1986).

Fig. 6: Map of Anglo-Saxon England.

Old English (*circa* AD 449–1100)

Old English is the vernacular Germanic language, the language of daily life, in Anglo-Saxon England from *circa* AD 449-1100, and is closely related to the main Teutonic language group. Its linguistic and literary development had its origins centuries before amongst Germanic peoples on the northern European mainland.[1]

Stylistic prose developed in English during the Old English period, when a major tradition of poetry was also formed. Alliterative prose and poetry were originally of oral composition, for the most part by skilled poets (*scopas*) and writers who may have developed or preserved a literary expression of observant formulaic form and diction; yet they produced literature that is original, stimulating, and beautiful. Literary composition most likely commenced shortly after the process of the conversion of the English to Christianity at the end of the seventh century, with monasteries providing a more focused approach to learning and manuscript production through their libraries and scriptoria. The earliest scriptorium of significance was at Lindisfarne in Northumbria; its achievements were firmly established by the venerable Bede. The greatest period of manuscript production in Anglo-Saxon England, however, was *circa* AD 950-1066, in the era of the Monastic Revival that was initiated by Dunstan, Archbishop of Canterbury (AD 909-988). Canterbury was renowned as the centre of Christianity in England from the end of the sixth century. It was during this period that such well-known literary collections as the Exeter Book and the Vercelli Book were produced.[2]

Anglo-Saxon is derived from West Germanic; there are two other such groups: East Germanic and North Germanic (see Fig. 7, p. 90).[3] One of the chief characteristics of this language group is that its speakers did not appear to pronounce consonants in the same way as most speakers of Indo-European languages. The German philologist, Jacob Grimm, was the first to articulate the fact that the Germanic languages are distinguished by certain consonant changes. This is known as Grimm's Law.[4] The following table adapted from Mitchell (1995), p. 11, illustrates some of the differences between Latin and Old English:

Latin	Old English	Modern English	Equivalents
piscis	*fisc*	*'fish'*	*p/f*
tres	*þreo*	*'three'*	*t/th*
centum	*hund*	*'hundred'*	*k/h*
genus	*cynn*	*'kin'*	*g/k*
decem	*tien*	*'ten'*	*d/t*

There are four principal distinguishable dialects of Old English: Northumbrian, Mercian, Kentish, and West Saxon. The differences are apparent in the spelling; it is otherwise difficult to categorize them. After *circa* A.D 900, West Saxon was increasingly used as a standard written language. Despite this, spelling conventions still displayed certain variations, even incorporating words from the other dialects, as is evident in the text of *The Dream of the Rood*, which is written in late West Saxon.

The most characteristic feature of Old English is its Englishness. Yet it does contain some important syntactical differences from English today. Two of the most notable of these are: (a) the frequent omission of the definite article, for example, *Ælfric feng to tun* ('Ælfric advanced to the town'), (b) the variation of the pattern of the subject, verb, object ('s.v.o.') pattern, which is now the standard pattern in modern English. Normally, Old English did use the 's.v.o.' order as in the example above; nevertheless, it did employ two further syntactical orders. One is where the verb has final position in the clause or sentence ('s.o.v'): e.g. *ac hie eft on hie fuhton* (449) ('but they afterwards against them fought'). The other is a verb subject ('v.s.') order as is used in many of the opening

---

[1] Introductions to Old English are Mitchell & Robinson (1992; repr. 1994), and Mitchell (1995), esp. pp. 17-72.

[2] A standard work on the history of Old English literature is Greenfield & Calder (1986).

[3] On the development of the English language, see Baugh & Cable (1978), and Algeo & Pyles (1982).

[4] On Grimm's Law, see Mitchell & Robinson (1992; repr. 1994), pp. 41-2, and Mitchell (1995), pp. 10-12.

entries throughout the *Anglo-Saxon Chronicle*: e.g. *981. Her on þis geare wæs Sancte Petroces stow forhergod* ('981. In this year Cornwall was ravaged').[5]

A major grammatical difference is that Old English changed the endings of nouns, adjectives, and pronouns, as did Latin, to indicate which words were the subject, object, genitive, etc. This use of inflections accounts for the greater fluidity of syntactical structure in Old English because meaning can be determined as much by inflections as by word order. In modern English inflections have been replaced by prepositions such as 'of', 'by', 'with', and so on.

The principal feature of Anglo-Saxon verse, to the forefront of refined literary expression, is for every line to divide into two half-lines which carry a minimum of four syllables. Two syllables in each half-line are stressed with the last of the main stresses in the first half-line requiring initial consonant alliterative correlation with the first emphasized stress in the second half-line; a caesura or pause separates each half-line.[6] The renowned Anglo-Saxon linguist, E. Sievers, illustrates that patterns of stress that appear in the half-line can be reduced to five or a possible six basic categories, though some variations can exist within this basic structure.[7]

In more recent times, T. C. Pope consolidates and interprets Old English versification in the light of Sievers's pioneering construction with conceptually disparate theoretical expression; he states that the verse was rhythmically regular rather than metrical.[8] There is evidence, even from *Beowulf*, that the performance of the poems was sometimes accompanied by the harp, making it probable that the verse had a regular rhythm; this rhythmic quality of Anglo-Saxon verse is more appreciated if the poetry is recited aloud. To evaluate the contributions of Sievers and Pope, both theories shed a great deal of light into the method and process of composition of Old English versification. Pope's emphasis on rhythmical regularity is particularly appealing in that its argument draws on the prose and the poetry; Ælfric's prose style in his Catholic Homilies is especially characterized by its rhythmic quality, as he formulated his prose from extant poetic traditions.[9]

The five basic metrical-types of Old English verse can be represented by the following illustration:[10]

Type A	´x ´x	(falling–falling)	gar to guþe (*The Battle of Maldon*, l. 13a)[11]
Type B	x ´x ´	(rising–rising)	wæs þæt beorhte bold (*Beowulf*, l. 997a)[12]
Type C	x ´´x	(clashing)	þær is blis mycel (*The Dream of the Rood*, l. 139b)
Type D₁	´´`x	(falling by stages)	healde his hordcofan (*The Wanderer*, l. 14a)[13]
Type D₂	´´x`	(broken fall)	hrim hrusan bond (*The Seafarer*, l. 32a)[14]
Type E	´`x´	(fall and rise)	feala ealra gebad (*The Dream of the Rood*, l. 125b)

---

[5] On Old English syntax and grammar, see Brunner (1965), Campbell (1959), Lass (1994), and Mitchel (1985).

[6] For introductions to the structure and form of Old English poetry, see Mitchell & Robinson (1992; repr. 1994), esp. pp. 161-7, and Mitchell (1995), esp. pp. 287-296. More detailed studies are in Cable (1991), Fulk (1992), Russom (1987), Sievers (1893), and Whitman (1993).

[7] Refer to Sievers (1893) and (1895).

[8] Pope (1942; repr. 1966).

[9] Ælfric's Catholic Homilies are edited in Thorpe (1884-6), Pope (1967-8), and Godden (1979).

[10] This diagram is adapted from Mitchell & Robinson (1992; repr. 1994), pp. 164-5, and Mitchell (1995), pp. 290-1.

[11] *The Battle of Maldon* is edited in Scragg & Deegen (1991).

[12] Editions of the epic *Beowulf* with *apparatus criticus* are in Wrenn & Bolton (1988; repr. 1992), & Chickering (1977; repr. 1989).

[13] *The Wanderer* is edited in Leslie (1985; repr. 1989).

[14] *The Seafarer* is edited in Gordon (1960; repr. 1964).

Such alliteration, where any combination of the five types is possible, was also employed to emphasize a chiasmus pattern. This is a figure of speech in which the order of the terms or images in the first two half-lines is reversed in the second two half-lines. The stress generally falls on the most important and keyword in each of the four half-lines that combine to form a chiasmus pattern. The following are good illustrations of this technique, taken from the Ruthwell runic poetic text:[15]

a   God Almehttig
b   modig fore allæ men
c   buga ic ni dorstæ
d   ac scealde fæstæ standa
d′   ahof ic riicnæ Kyninc
c′   hælda ic ni dorstæ
b′   bismæradu ungket men
a′   guman

The focus in a and a′ is on the two natures of Jesus as God and man, in b and b′ what man saw and what man did, in c and c′ what the cross dared not do, and in d and d′ what the cross did. In this chiasmus the theme is the Crucifixion.

The frequent use of compound words is another feature of Old English poetry. Some make statements as in the case of the following examples from *The Dream*: 'holmwudu', l. 91a ('hill wood'), 'middangearde', l. 104a ('world'), 'sigebeam', 127a ('cross'), 'Heahfædere', l. 134b ('God the Father'). Others are condensed comparisons, for instance, Hælendes treow (l. 25a) / wudu selesta (l. 27a) ('Saviour's tree' / 'best of woods'). This use in *The Dream* both consolidates and expands the image of the cross, for it associates it with Christ (divine) and its natural origin (nature). While yet others function as kennings, compressed metaphors in which 'a' is compared to 'b' without 'b' the point of comparison being made explicit. The metaphor 'The camel is the ship of the desert' would become the kenning 'The desert ship lurched on'. So the sea is *hwæl-weg* (m.) 'whale-way', a ship *yþ-hengest* (m.) 'wave-horse', and a ministral *hleahtor-smiþ* (m.) 'laughter-smith' – these examples are taken for the Old English epic *Beowulf*.[16]

An associated convention is periphrasis, a roundabout way of referring to something by means of several words instead of naming the signifier directly with a single word or phrase. More generally referred to as circumlocution, periphrasis is frequently employed in Old English poetry as euphemisms for the sea, death, etc. It can also have a more dramatic effect than the use of kennings as can be seen in the following example *ond he hine ðær hwile reste*, l. 64b ('and he rested himself there for a while', i.e., he is dead), from *The Dream*.

Occasionally Old English poets shift in the course of a poem to an expanded form of verse that is termed hypermetric. Hypermetric verses have three rather than two accented syllables in each half-line; they seem to be composed of a regular verse-type with another half-line added on, as can be seen in ll. 59-69 of *The Dream*. Hypermetric lines usually occur in groups like this, and, through such a special effect, indicate to the Anglo-Saxon audience the thematic importance of such passages.

Rhyme has no functional role in Anglo-Saxon versification to demarcate the boundaries of verses or provide ornamentation; these functions are served by alliteration. The Anglo-Saxons did not know rhyme, but in later Old English poetry there are signs that rhyme is beginning to displace alliteration as a functional device. This can be seen in ll. 271 and 282 of *The Battle of Maldon*, where rhyme rather than alliteration links the two half-lines.[17] Such lines anticipate the Middle English period, when rhyme displaces alliteration almost completely.

---

[15] For further discussion on this example from the Ruthwell Cross, see Howlett in Cassidy (1992), pp. 88-90.

[16] See Note 12.

[17] See Note 11.

The final characteristic of Old English poetry of significance with regard to the texts in this edition is the use of formulae: set metrical combinations vary according to the pattern of alliteration. Many of these set phrases derive directly from an oral tradition and Christian poets like of *The Dream of the Rood* have adapted them for use in their literary verse. A good illustration of this convention is the repeated use of the phrase 'Men þa leofstan' at l. 95 & l. 100 of *The Dream*. This is the most commonly used formula throughout Anglo-Saxon prose preaching texts, and provides important evidence here for the didactic function of this poem.

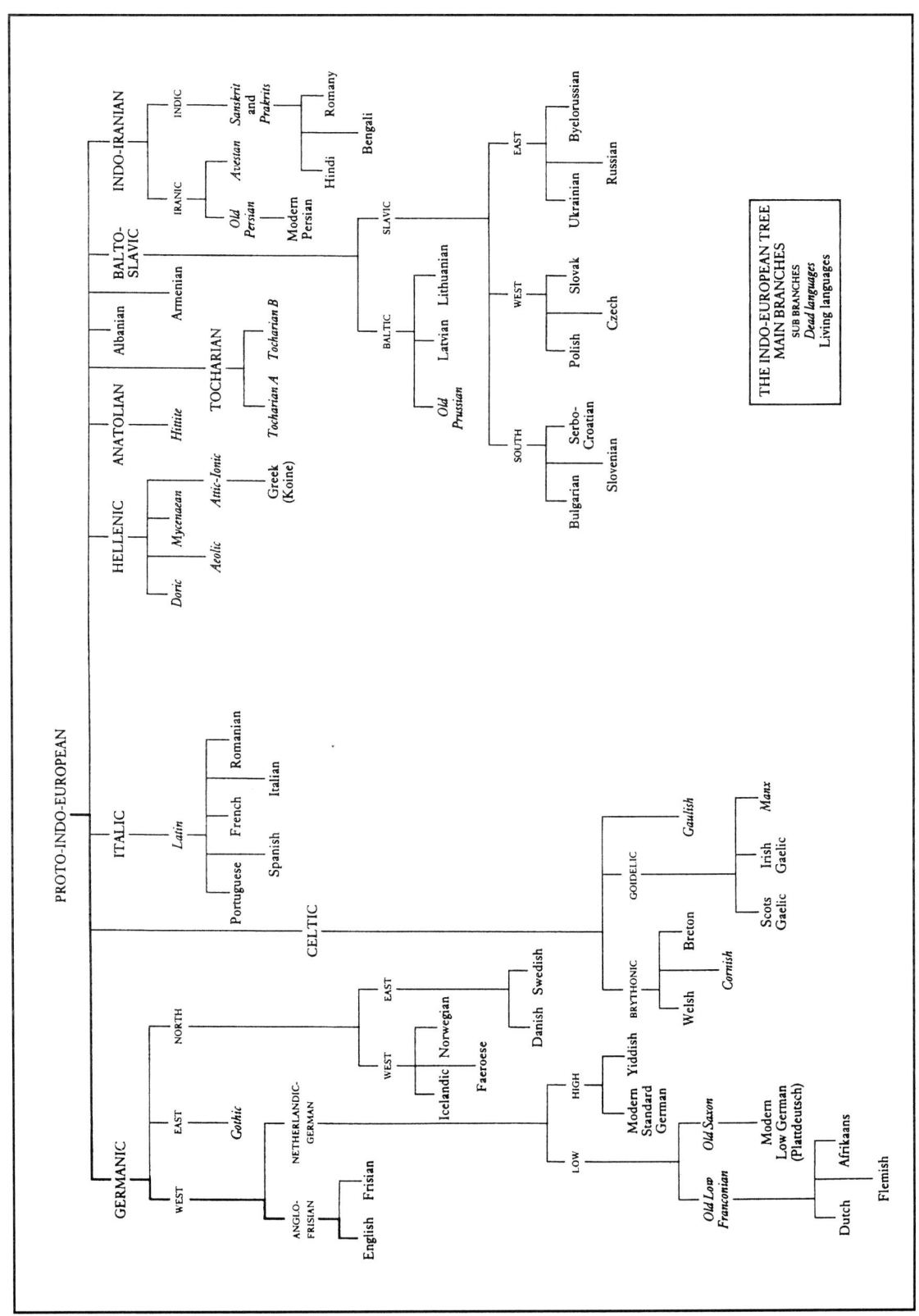

Fig. 7: Indo-European Language Tree

© Harcourt Brace & Company, reproduced by permission of the publisher
from Pyles & Algeo (1982), eds., *The Origins and Development of the English Language,* Third Edition.

Table 1

Artefacts & Literature of Anglo-Saxon England

This table records the principal literary and artistic achievements of the Anglo-Saxon period. The date or approximate date is recorded in the left-hand column followed by a brief description of the nature of the literary or artistic work.

circa 540	Gildas in *De Excidio Britanniae* laments the effects of the Germanic settlements on the Britons
circa 625	Ship-burial at Sutton Hoo, Suffolk (mound 1)
634	King Oswald raises a wooden cross on the eve of battle and his victory over Cædwalla, King of the Britons
circa 653	The first stone churches are built in the south-east; to the north later in the seventh century Benedict Biscop employs masons and glaziers for the establishment of monasteries at Monkwearmouth and Jarrow; not until towards the end of the Anglo-Saxon period are churches in stone common
657-80	Cædmon uses Germanic alliterative forms for religious verse
circa 690	The oak coffin of St. Cuthbert is incised
circa 700	The Lindisfarne Gospels are written and decorated
circa 730	The Franks Casket, carved of whalebone, bears biblical and secular Germanic narrative panels surrounded largely by runic inscriptions
731	Bede completes his *Ecclesiastical History of the English People*
circa 730-50	The Ruthwell Cross is carved and erected; the Bewcastle Cross was carved and erected possibly some years earlier
796	Nennius writes/revises the *Historia Brittonum*
circa 830	The Book of Kells, Celtic illuminated Gospels, is completed
circa 878	The Ælfred Jewel; gold plate encloses a small green figure bearing flowered sceptres against an oval blue rock crystal background. Its short Anglo-Saxon inscription attributes patronage to King Ælfred
circa 886	King Ælfred's translations into Anglo-Saxon are initiated. Also the period of the beginnings of the *Anglo-Saxon Chronicle*
circa 971	The Blickling Homilies
circa 950-1000	The approximate dates for the major poetry codices (Junius MS 11 Vercelli Book, Exeter Book, and the Beowulf MS)
990-2	Ælfric begins his series of Catholic Homilies
993-8	Ælfric's Lives of the Saints
circa 1014	Wulfstan's *Sermo Lupi ad Anglos*
circa 1074	The Bayeux Tapestry is embroidered soon after the Norman Conquest, celebrating its victory
circa 1100	The Brussels Cross

Table 2

Chronological Table of the Anglo-Saxon Period

This table records the principal military, political, and religious historical events that took place during the Anglo-Saxon period. The date or approximate date is recorded in the left-hand column followed by a brief description of the historical event.

from *circa* 400	Germanic people settle in Britain
597	St. Augustine arrives in Kent to convert the English to Christianity
616	Death of Æthelberht, King of Kent
633	Death of Edwin, King of Northumbria
634	Bishop Aidan established at Lindisfarne
642	Death of Oswald, King of Northumbria
664	Synod of Whitby
669	Archbishop Theodore and Abbot Hadrian arrive in Canterbury
674	Monastery at Monkwearmouth founded
682	Monastery at Jarrow founded
687	Death of St. Cuthbert
689	Death of Cædwalla, King of Wessex
690	Death of Archbishop Theodore
709	Deaths of Bishops Wilfrid and Aldhelm
716-57	Æthelbald is King of Mercia
735	Death of St. Bede
754	Death of St. Boniface, Anglo-Saxon missionary to Germany
757-96	Offa is King of Mercia
781	Alcuin of York meets Charlemagne in Parma and thereafter leaves York for continental Europe
793	The Vikings attack Lindisfarne
802-39	Ecgberht is King of Wessex
804	Death of Alcuin
839-56	Æthelwulf is King of Wessex
869	The Vikings defeat and kill Edmund, King of East Anglia
871-99	Alfred the Great is King of Wessex
878	Alfred defeats the Viking army at the battle of Edington, and the Vikings settle in East Anglia (AD 879-80)
899-924	Edward the Elder is King of Wessex
924-39	Athelstan is King of Wessex and the first King of all England

937	Battle of Brunanburh: Athelstan defeats an alliance of Scots and Scandinavians
957-75	Edgar is King of England
959-88	Dunstan is Archbishop of Canterbury
963-84	Æthelwold is Bishop of Winchester
964	Secular clerics are expelled from the Old Minster at Winchester and replaced by monks
971-92	Oswald is Archbishop of York
973	King Edgar is crowned at Bath
978-1016	Æthelred 'the Unready' is King of England
985-7	Abbo of Fleury is at Ramsey
991	The Battle of Maldon: the Vikings defeat an English army led by Byrhtnoth
circa 1010	Death of Ælfric, Abbot of Eynsham
1013	The English submit to Swein, King of Denmark
1016-35	Cnut is King of England
1023	Death of Wulfstan, Archbishop of York
1042-66	Edward the Confessor is King of England
1066	The Norman Conquest: the English army led by Harold is defeated by William the Conqueror at the Battle of Hastings

Table 3

Contents of the Vercelli Book

Column 1 refers to the number of the individual texts as they appear in the Vercelli Book; Column 2 identifies whether they are prose or poetic in style; Column 3 presents the manuscript rendition of the texts as titled or untitled, followed by a brief description of their thematic content, or as in the case of the poetry the titles assigned by editors; and column 4 cites their particular folio and line numbers within the manuscript.

1	Homily I	[Beginning damaged] Treatise on the Paschus	fols 2r.1 – 9r.24
2	Homily II	[Untitled] Eschatological treatise on *De Die Iudicii* (Doomsday)	fols. 9v.1 – 12r.24
3	Homily III	[Untitled] Penitential text for Lent	fols. 12v.2 – 16r.18
4	Homily IV	[Untitled] Eschatological treatise on the approach of Doomsday	fols. 16v.2 – 24v.14
5	Homily V	'To Middanwintra. *Ostende Nobis Domine*' Treatise on the Nativity	fols. 25r.1 – 29r.10
6	Poetry I	*Andreas*	fols. 29v.1 – 52v.9
7	Poetry II	*Fates of the Apostles*	fols.52v.10 – 54r.19
8	Homily VI	'Incipit Narrare Miracula Que Facta Fuerant Ante Aduentum Saluatoris Domini Nostri Iesu Christi' A further Treatise on the Nativity	fols. 54v.1 – 56r.23
9	Homily VII	[Untitled, except for the numeral 'ii'] A Treatise on Immoral Behaviour	fols. 56r.23 – 59r.1
10	Homily VIII	[Untitled, except for the numeral 'iii'] Eschatological piece on Christ as Judge	fols. 59r.2 – 61r.12
11	Homily IX	[Untitled, except for the numeral 'iiii'] Eschatological explanation of the signs of the termination of all	fols. 61r.13 – 65r.17
12	Homily X	[Untitled, except for the numeral 'v'] Eschatological treatise on the way to salvation	fols. 65r.18 – 71r.10

13	Homily XI	'Spel to Forman Gangdæge' Rogation Text I	fols. 71v.1 – 73v.15
14	Homily XII	'Spel to Oðrum Gangdæge' Rogation Text II	fols. 73v.16 – 75v.6
15	Homily XIII	'Spel to Þriddan Gangdæge' Rogation Text III	fols. 75v.7 – 76v.8
16	Homily XIV	'Larspel to Swylcere Tide swa Man Wile' Ascension Text	fols. 76v.8 – 80v.6
17	Homily XV	'Alia Omelia De Die Iudicii' Eschatological	fols. 80v.8 – 85v.6
18	Homily XVI	'Omelia Epyffania Domini' Epiphany (6 Jan.)	fols. 85v.8 – 90v.20
19	Homily XVII	'De Purificatione Sancta[e] Maria[e]' Candlemas (2 Feb.)	fols. 90v.22 – 94v.22
20	Homily XVIII	'De Sancto Martino Confessore' Life of St. Martin of Tours	fols. 94v.24 – 101r.17
21	Poetry III	*Body & Soul I*	fols. 101v.1 – 103v.24
22	Poetry IV	*Homiletic fragment I*	fols. 104r.1 – 104v.5
23	Poetry V	*The Dream of the Rood*	fols. 104v.6 – 106r.24
24	Homily XIX	[Untitled] Rogation Text	fols. 106v.2 – 109v.9
25	Homily XX	[Untitled] Rogation Text	fols. 109v.13 – 112r.9
26	Homily XXI	[Untitled] Rogation Text	fols. 112r.14 – 116v.18
27	Homily XXII	[Untitled] Spiritual Meditation	fols. 116v.20 – 120v.17
28	Poetry VI	*Elene* (Story of the finding of the Cross)	fols. 121r.1 – 133v.6
29	Homily XXIII	[Untitled] Life of St. Guthlac	fols. 133v.7 – 135v.28

Table 4

Early Cross-Type Representations

(1)   The equilateral cross is called *crux quadrata* or Greek cross. Its equal arms intersect at right angles.

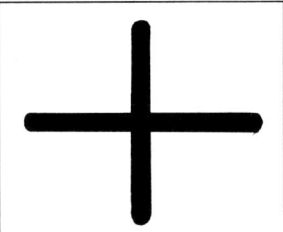

(2)   The St. Andrew's cross or *crux decrussata* has equal arms represented obliquely at right angles, contrasting but similar to the vertical-horizontal intersection in (1) and resembling the symbolism of the Greek initial 'Chi' and the Latin numeral 'X'.

(3)   The *crux commissa* resembles the symbolism of the Greek initial 'Tau' and the Latin initial 'T'.

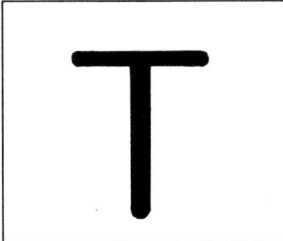

(4)   The *crux immissa* or Latin cross has the horizontal transept intersecting the vertical shaft one-third the distance from the top.

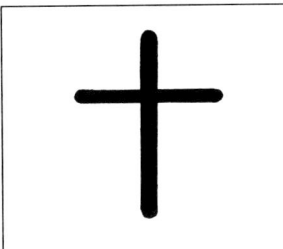

(5)   The gammadion, *crux gammata* or swastika (Sanskrit) is an equilateral cross with four intersecting Greek capital initials, *gammas*, which are joined at right angles and revolving to the right. Occasionally they are displayed reversed and revolving to the left.

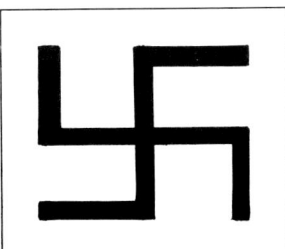

(6)   A *tau* cross surmounted by an oval loop is known as *crux ansata, ankh* or handled cross. It is synonymous with the Egyptian hieroglyph, *ankh*, which means 'life'.

These cross diagrams are adaptations from P. C Finney's account of the evolution of the cross in Ferguson (1997; repr. 1999).

Fig. 8: Reading in a Monastic Setting.
The monk here is reading from the Scriptures. (Drawing by David Rooney).
© The O'Brien Press, Dublin.

Select Bibliography
& Glossary

Select Bibliography

This bibliography is not intended to be comprehensive; its purpose is rather to cite publications on the Ruthwell Cross, *The Dream of the Rood* and the Brussels Cross, and/or to provide access to more extensive bibliographies. It is hoped that the reader may find these works of use for further research and study. Publications with bibliographies of added or particular importance are marked with an asterisk (*). The bibliography is divided into two sections: (a) Texts, Editions, & Primary Sources, and (b) General Studies. All abbreviations used are expanded in the List of Abbreviations (pp. x-xi).

Texts, Editions, & Primary Sources

ANDERSON, A. O., & **ANDERSON**, M. O. (1961; repr. 1991), ed. & trans., *Adomnán's Life of Columba* (Edinburgh).

ANDRIEU, M. (1931-61), *Les Ordines Romani du Haut Moyen Age*, 5 Vols (Louvain).

AVONTO, L. (1973), ed., *L'Ospedale di S. Brigida degli Scoti e il 'Vercelli Book'* (Vercelli, Italy).

BAILEY, R. N., & **CRAMP**, R. (1988), eds., *Corpus of Anglo-Saxon Stone Sculpture in England, Cumberland, Westmorland and Lancashire-North-of-the-Sands*, Vol. II (Oxford).

BOSWORTH, J., & **TOLLER**, T. N., (1882-98), eds., *An Anglo-Saxon Dictionary* (Oxford); **TOLLER**, T. N. (1908-21), ed., *An Anglo-Saxon Dictionary . . . Supplement* (Oxford); & **CAMPBELL**, A. (1972), ed., *An Anglo-Saxon Dictionary . . . Enlarged Addenda and Corrigenda* (Oxford).

BRADLEY, S. A. J. (1982), ed., *Anglo-Saxon Poetry* (London).

BRETT, M., **BROOKS**, C. N. L., & **WHITELOCK**, D. (1981), eds., *Councils and Synods: 871–1066* (Part I) (Oxford).

BRUNNER, K. (1965), *Altenglische Grammatik nach der angelsächsischen Grammatik von Eduard Sievers*, Third Edition (Tübingen).

CALDER, D. G., et al. (1983), eds., *Sources and Analogues of Old English Poetry II: The Major Germanic and Celtic Texts in Translation* (Cambridge).

CAMERON, A., et al. (1983), eds., *Old English Word Studies: A Preliminary Author and Word Index* (Toronto).

CAMERON, A., **AMOS**, A. C., & **HEALEY**, A. diP. (1986–), eds., *The Dictionary of Old English* (Toronto).

CAMPBELL, A. (1959), *Old English Grammar* (Oxford).

CARBOL, F., & **LECLERC**, H. (1907-50), eds., *Dictionnaire d'archéologie Chrétienne et de liturgie*, 15 Vols. (Paris).

CARNEY, J. (1964; repr. 1989), ed. & trans., *The Poems of Blathmac, Son of Cú Brettan*, Irish Texts Society, Vol. XLVII (Dublin).

CHAMBERS, R., **FÖRSTER**, M., & **FLOWER**, R. (1933), eds., *The Exeter Book of Old English Poetry* (London).

CHICKERING, H. D. (1977; repr. 1989), ed., *Beowulf* (New York).

CLARK HALL, J. R. (1970), *A Concise Anglo-Saxon Dictionary*, Fourth Edition with a supplement by H. D. **MERITT** (Cambridge).

COLGRAVE, B., & **MYNORS**, R. A. B. (1969), ed. & trans., *Bede's Ecclesiastical History of the English People* (Oxford).

COOK, A. S. (1905), ed., *The Dream of the Rood* (Oxford).

CRAMP, R. (1984), ed., *Corpus of Anglo-Saxon Stone Sculpture in England, County Durham and Northumberland*, Vol. I (2 Parts) (Oxford).

CROSSLEY-HOLLAND, K. (1984; repr. 1991), ed., *The Anglo-Saxon World: An Anthology* (Oxford).

CROSSLEY-HOLLAND, K., & **MITCHELL**, B. (1965), eds., *The Battle of Maldon and Other Old English Poems* (London).

CUBITT, C. (1995), ed., *Anglo-Saxon Church Councils c. 650-c. 850* (New York & London).

DAVIES, J. G. (1972; repr. 1978), ed., *A Dictionary of Liturgy & Worship* (London).

DICKENS, B., & **ROSS**, A. S. C. (1934), eds., *The Dream of the Rood* (London).

DOBBIE, E. V. K. (1942), ed., *Anglo-Saxon Minor Poems*, ASPR, VI (New York).

DOUGLAS, D. C. (1979), ed., *English Historical Documents*, Second Edition (London). Vol. I, covering the years 500-1042, edited by D. Whitelock.

EARLE, J., & **PLUMMER**, C. (1892-9), eds., *Two of the Anglo-Saxon Chronicles Parallel* (Oxford).

FÖRSTER, M. (1913), ed., *Il Codice Vercellese con Omelie e Poesie in Lingua Anglosassone* (Rome).

GARMONSWAY, G. N. (1953; repr. 1972), ed., *The Anglo-Saxon Chronicle* (London).

GODDEN, M. R. (1979), ed., *Ælfric's Catholic Homilies: The Second Series*, EETS ss 5 (London).

GOLLANCZ, I. (1927), ed., *The Cædmon Manuscript of Anglo-Saxon Poetry* (London).

GORDEN, E. V. (1976), ed., *The Battle of Maldon* (Manchester). Supplement by D. G. Scragg.

GORDEN, I. (1960; repr. 1964), ed., *The Seafarer* (London).

GREENFIELD, S. B., & **ROBINSON***, F. C. (1980), eds., *A Bibiography of Publications on Old English Literature to the End of 1972* (Toronto & Manchester).

GRÉGOIRE, R. (1966), ed., *Les Homéliares du Moyen Age* (Rome).

HAMER, R. (1970; repr. 1981), ed., *A Choice of Anglo-Saxon Verse* (London).

HADDAN, A. W., & **STUBBS**, W. (1871), eds., *Councils and Ecclesiastical Documents relating to Great Britain and Ireland*, Vol. III (Oxford).

HOOPS, J. (1911-9), *Reallexikon der germanischen Altertumskunde* (Strasbourg).

JAMES, M. R. (1953), ed., *The Apocryphal New Testament* (Oxford).

KEISER, A. (1919), *The influence of Christianity on the Vocabulary of Old English Poetry* (Urbana).

KELLER, W. (1906), *Angelsächsische Palaeographie* (Berlin).

KENNEDY, C. W. (1910), ed., *The Poems of Cynewulf* (London).

KENNEDY, C. W. (1952), ed., *Early English Christian Poetry* (London).

KER, N. R. (1950), 'C. Maier's Transcript of the Vercelli Book', *Medium Aevum*, XIX, pp. 17–25.

KER*, N. R. (1957), ed., *Catalogue of Manuscripts Containing Anglo-Saxon* (Oxford).

KRAPP, G. P. (1932), ed., *The Vercelli Book* (New York).

LESLIE, R. Y. (1966; repr. 1989), ed., *The Wanderer* (Exeter).

LIEBERMANN, F. (1903-16), ed., *Die Gesetze der Angelsachsen*, 3 Vols. (Halle).

McKENZIE, J. L. (1966; repr. 1975), ed., *Dictionary of the Bible* (London).

MAGOUN, F. P., & **WALKER**, J. A. (1950), eds., *An Old English Anthology* (Dubuque, Iowa).

MAIER, C. (1834), ed., *Beschreibung des Codex Capitulare Vercellensis, n. CXVII* (Lincoln's Inn MS. Misc. 312).

MALONE, K. (1963), ed., *The Nowell Codex: British Museum Cotton Vitellius A. XV, Second MS*, EEMF, Vol. XII (Copenhagen).

MEEHAN, D. (1958), ed. & trans., *Adamnan's De Loctis Sanctis*, Scriptores Latini Hiberniae, 3 (Dublin).

MIGNE, J. P. (1844-64), ed., *Patrologiae Cursus Completus, Series Latina* (Paris).

MIGNE, J. P. (1857-1912), ed., *Patrologiae Cursus Completus, Series Graeca* (Paris).

MITCHELL, B. (1985), *Old English Syntax*, Vols. I & II (Oxford).

MITCHELL*, B. (1990), ed., *A Critical Bibliography of Old English Syntax* (Oxford).

MORRIS, R. (1871), ed., *Legend of the Holy Rood: Symbols of the Passion-Cross*, EETS os 46 (London).

MORRIS, R. (1874, 1876, 1880; repr. 1967), ed., *The Blickling Homilies*, EETS os 58, 63, & 73 (London).

MURPHY, G. (1956; repr. 1998), ed., *Early Irish Lyrics: 8th -12th Century* (Oxford & Dublin).

NAPIER, A. S. (1900), *Old English Glosses* (Oxford).

PLUMMER, C. (1896), ed., *Venerabilis Baedae Opera Historica*, 2 Vols. (Oxford).

POPE, J. C. (1967-8), ed., *Homilies of Ælfric: A Supplementary Collection*, EETS os 259-60 (London).

ROSENTHAL*, J. T. (1985), ed., *Anglo-Saxon History: An Annotated Bibliography 450-1066* (New York).

SCRAGG, D. G. (1992), ed., *The Vercelli Homilies*, EETS os 300 (London).

SCRAGG, D. G., & **DEEGEN**, M. (1991), eds., *The Battle of Maldon AD 991* (Oxford).

SEYMOUR, M. C. (1965), ed., *Translations from Old English* (Edinburgh).

SHIPPEY, T. A. (1972), ed., *Old English Verse* (London).

SISAM, C. (1976), ed., *The Vercelli Book*, EEMF, Vol. XIX (Copenhagen).

STOKES, W. (1905; repr. 1984), ed. & trans., *The Martyrology of Oengus the Culdee*, Henry Bradshaw Society, XXIX (London).

SWANTON, M. (1975; repr. 1993), ed. & trans., *Anglo-Saxon Prose* (London).

SWANTON*, M. (1987; repr. 1992), ed., *The Dream of the Rood* (Exeter) (New Edition 1996).

SYMNONS, T. (1953), ed., *Regularis Concordia: Angliae Nationis Monachorum Sanctimonialiumque* (London).

THORPE, B. (1844-6), ed., *The Homilies of the Anglo-Saxon Church* (London).

VIVES, J. (1963), ed., *Concilios Visigoticos e Hispano-Romanos*, Consejo Superior de Investigaciones Cientificas, Instituto Enrique Flores (Barcelona).

WALPOLE, A. S. (1922), ed., *Early Latin Hymns* (Cambridge).

WRENN, C. L., & **BOLTON**, W. F. (1988; repr. 1992), eds., *Beowulf*, Revised Edition (Exeter).

WÜLCKER, R. P. (1885), *Grundriss zur Geschichte der angelsächsischen Literatur mit einer übersicht der angelsächsischen Sprachissenschaft* (Leipzig).

WÜLCKER, R. P. (1894), ed., *Die Verceller Handschrift, die Handschrift des Cambridger Corpus Christi College CCI, die Gedichte der sogen. Caedmonhandschrift, Judith, der Hymnus Caedmons, Heiligenkalender nebst kleineren geistlichen Dichtungen* (Bibliothek der angelsächsischen Poesie, 2) (Leipzig).

WÜLFING, J. E. (1894-1901), *Die Syntax in den Werken Alfreds des Grossen*, 2 Vols. (Bonn).

WÜLFING, J. E., & **WRIGHT**, T. (1884), eds., *Anglo-Saxon and Old English Vocabularies*, Second Edition, 2 Vols. (London).

General Works

ADAMSON, S., **LAW**, V., **VINCENT**, N., & **WRIGHT**, S. (1990), eds., *Paper form the Fifth International Conference on English Historical Linguistics, Cambridge, 6-9 April 1987* (Amsterdam & Philadelphia).

ALEGO, J., & **PYLES**, T. (1982), *The Origins and Development of the English Language*, Third Edition (San Diego).

ALEXANDER, J. J. G. (1978), *Insular Manuscripts, 6th to the 9th Century* (London).

ALLEN, J. R., & **ANDERSON**, J. (1903; repr. 1993), *Early Cross Monuments of Scotland* (Edinburgh; repr. Angus).

ALLEN, M. J. B., & **CALDER**, D. G. (1976), *Sources and Analogues of Old English Poetry: The Major Texts in Translation* (Totowa).

BALDWIN BROWN, G. (1921), *The Arts in Early England. The Ruthwell and Bewcastle Crosses, the Gospels of Lindisfarne and Other Christian Monuments, with Philological Chapters by A. Blyth Webster* (London).

BARASCH, M. (1992), *Icon Studies in the History of an Idea* (New York).

BARNES, T. D. (1981), *Constantine and Eusebius* (Cambridge, Mass.).

BAUER, A. (1890), *Ueber die Sprache und Mundart der altenglischen Dichtungen Andreas, Gûðlác, Phönix, hl. Kreuz und Höllenfahrt Cristi* (Marburg).

BAUGH, A. C., & **CABLE**, T. (1978), *A History of the English Language*, Third Edition (Englewood Cliffs, N. J., & London).

BECKWITH, J. (1961), *The Art of Constantinople: An Introduction to Byzantine Art* (London).

BELTING, H. (1994), *Likeness and Presence: A History of the Image before the Era of Art*. Trans. by E. Jephott (London & Chicago).

BENNETT, S. A. J. (1982), *Poetry of the Passion: Studies in Twelve Centuries of English Verse* (Oxford).

BERKHOUT, C. T. (1974), 'The Problem of OE Holmwudu', *Mediaeval Studies*, XXXVI, pp. 429-33.

BLACKHOUSE, J., **TURNER**, D. H., & **WEBSTER**, L. (1984), eds., *The Golden Age of Anglo-Saxon Art 966-1066* (London).

BLUHME, F. (1824-36), *Ledenden oder Homilien in angelsäxischer Sprache* (Halle).

BOENIG, R. (1985), 'The *engel dryhtnes* and Mimesis in *The Dream of the Rood*', *NM*, LXXXVI, pp. 442-6.

BOLTON, W. F. (1959–60), 'Connectives in *The Seafarer* and *The Dream of the Rood*, *MP*, 57, pp. 260–2.

BOLTON, W. F. (1964) 'Tatwine's *De Cruce Christi* and *The Dream of the Rood*', Archiv., CC, pp. 344-6.

BOLTON, W. F. (1976), '*The Dream of the Rood* 9b: 'Engel' = *Nuntius*?', *N & Q* , 213, pp. 165–6.

BOLTON, W. F. (1980), 'The Book of Job in *The Dream of the Rood*', *MÆ*, VI, pp. 87-103.

BORGOGNONE, F. (1951), *Il Problema del Vercelli Book* (Alessandria).

BOSSE, R. B., et al. (1984), eds., *Proceedings of the Illinois Medieval Association* (Macomb., Illinois).

BRASWELL, B. K. (1978), '*The Dream of the Rood* and Aldhelm on Sacred Prosopopoeia', *MS*, 40, pp. 461–7.

BRITTON, G. C. (1967), '*Bealuwara Weorc* in *The Dream of the Rood*', *NM*, LXVIII, pp. 273-6.

BROWN, G. B. (1921), *The Arts of Early England*, V, (London).

BROWN, G. B., & **LETHABY**, W. R. (1913), 'The Bewcastle and Ruthwell Crosses', *BM*, XXIII, pp. 43-9.

BROWN, G. B., & **WEBSTER**, A. B. (1920), *Royal Commission on Ancient and Historical Monuments . . . of Scotland*, vii, *County of Dumfries* (Edinburgh).

BROWN, M. (1991), *Anglo-Saxon Manuscripts* (London).

BROWN, M. (1994), *Understanding Illuminated Manuscripts: A Guide to Technical Terms* (Malibu & London).

BROWN, P. R., **CRAMPTON**, G. R., & **ROBINSON**, F. C. (1986), eds., *Modes of Interpretation in Old English Literature. Essays in Honor of Stanley B. Greenfield* (Toronto).

BROWNE, G. F. (1916), *The Ancient Cross Shafts at Bewcastle and Ruthwell* (Cambridge).

BRUCE-MITFORD, R. L. S. (1968; repr. 1972), *The Sutton Hoo Burial: A Handbook*, Second Edition (London).

BRUCE-MITFORD, R. L. S. (1975, 1978, 1983), *The Sutton Hoo Ship-Burial*, 3 Vols. (London).

BUNDI, A. (1979), 'Per la ricostruzione dei passi frammentari dell'iscrizone runica della Croce di Ruthwell', *Annali Istituto Universitario Orientale Napoli: Filologia Germanica*, XXII, pp. 21-58.

BURLIN, R. B. (1968), 'The Dream of the Rood and the *Vita Contemplativa*', *SP*, LXV, pp. 23-43.

BURROW, J. A. (1959; repr. 1968), 'An Approach to *The Dream of the Rood*', *Neophil.*, 43, pp. 123–33. Reprinted in **STEVENS**, M., & **MANDEL**, J. (1968), eds., *Old English Literature* (Lincoln), pp. 253-67.

BÜTOW, H. (1935), *Das Altenglische 'Traumgesicht vom Kreuz'* (Heidelberg).

CABLE, T. (1991), *The English Alliterative Tradition* (Philadelphia).

CAMPBELL, J. (1982; repr. 1991), *The Anglo-Saxons* (London).

CANUTESON, J. (1969), 'The Crucifixion and The Second Coming in *The Dream of the Rood*', *MP*, LXVI, pp. 293-7.

CASSIDY*, B (1992), ed., *The Ruthwell Cross: Papers from the Colloquium Sponsored by the Index of Christian Art, Princeton University, 8 December 1989* (Princeton).

CHASE, C. L. (1980), '*Christ III, The Dream of the Rood*, and early Christian Passion Piety', *Viator*, XI, pp. 11-33.

CHERNISS, M. D. (1973), 'The Cross as Christ's Weapon: the Influence of Heroic Literary Tradition on *The Dream of the Rood*', *ASE*, II, pp. 241-52.

CLAYTON, M. (1985), 'Homiliaries and Preaching in Anglo-Saxon England', *Peritia. Journal of the Medieval Academy of Ireland*, IV, pp. 207-42.

CLAYTON, M. (1990), *The Cult of the Virgin Mary in Anglo-Saxon England,* Cambridge Studies in Anglo-Saxon England, 2 (Cambridge).

CLELAND, J. H. (1979), 'The Art of The Dream of the Rood', *Faith & Reason*, Vol.II, pp. 3-25.

COLLINGWOOD, W. G. (1918), 'The Ruthwell Cross and Its Relationship to Other Monuments', *Trans. Dumfries and Galloway Antiquarian Society*, S3, v, pp. 34-84.

COLLINGWOOD, W. G. (1927), *Northumbrian Crosses in the Pre-Norman Age* (London).

COLLINS*, R. (1991), *Early Medieval Europe 300-1000* (London).

CONNELLY, J. (1972; repr. 1978), 'Ember Days' in **DAVIES** (1972; repr. 1978), pp. 168-9.

CONNELLY, J. (1972; repr. 1978), 'Rogation Days' in **DAVIES** (1972; repr. 1978), pp. 336-7.

COOK, A. S. (1888), *Cardinal Guala and the Vercelli Book* (Sacramento).

COOK, A. S. (1915), 'The Date of the Old English Inscription on the Brussels Cross', *MLR,* X, pp.157-61.

CRAMP, R. J. (1959-60), 'The Anglian Sculptured Crosses of Dumfrieshire', *Trans. Dumfries and Galloway Antiquarian Society*, S3, XXXVIII, pp. 9-20.

CRAMP, R. J. (1965), *Early Northumbrian Sculpture* (Jarrow Lecture, 1965), (Jarrow).

CRAMP, R. J. (1995), *Whithorn and the Northumbrian Expansion Westwards* (Third Whithorn Lecture, 17 September 1994), (Whithorn).

CRAMP, R. J. (1997), 'The Insular Tradition: An Overview' in **KARKOV, RYAN, & FARRELL** (1997), p. 295.

CREED, R. P. (1967), ed., *Old English Poetry* (Providence).

CROSSLEY-HOLLAND, K. (1994), *The Anglo-Saxon World* (Woodbridge, Suffolk).

d'ARDENNE, S. T. R. O. (1939), 'The Old English Inscription on the Brussels Cross', *English Studies*, XXI, pp. 145–64, 271–2.

DAS, S. K. (1942), *Cynewulf and the Cynewulf Canon* (Calcutta).

DEERING, W. (1890), *The Anglo-Saxon Poets on the Judgement Day* (Halle).

de GRÉGORY, Ed. G. (1819-24), *Isoria della Vercellese Letteratura ed Arti* (Turin).

de LUBAC, H. (1959-64), *Exégèse médiévale, le quatre sens de l'Ecriture*, Vols. 1-4. (Paris).

DIAMOND, R. E. (1958), 'Heroic Diction in *The Dream of the Rood*' in **WALLACE & ROSS** (1958), pp. 3-7.

DICKINS, B. (1932), 'A System of Transliteration for Old English Runic Inscriptions', *Leeds Studies in English*, I, pp. 15-19.

DILLON, M., & **CHADWICK**, N. (1967), *The Celtic Realms* (London), pp. 270-3.

DINWIDDIE, J. L. (1927), *The Ruthwell Cross and Its Story* (Dumfries).

DODWELL, C. R. (1982), *Anglo-Saxon Art. A New Perspective* (Ithaca & Manchester).

DOLCETTI CORAZZA, V. (1999), ed., *Vercelli tra Oriente ed Occidente, tra tarda antichità e medioevo* (Alessandria, Italy).

DUBS, K. E. (1975), '*Hæleð*: Heroism in The Dream of the Rood', *Neophil*, LIX, pp. 614-5.

DUCKETT, E. S. (1965), *Alfred the Great: The King and His England* (Chicago).

DUMVILLE, D. N. (1993), *English Caroline Script and Monastic History: Studies in Benedictinism, AD 950-1030* (Woodbridge, Suffolk).

DUNLOP, C. (1932), *Processions* (London).

EBERT, A. (1884), 'Über das angelsächsische Gedicht *Der Traum vom heiligen Kreuze*', *Berichte über die Verhandlungen der königlich sächsischen Gesellschaft der Wissenschaften zu Leipzig*, Phil.- Hist. Classe, XXXVI, pp. 81-93.

EDWARDS, R. R. (1970), 'Narrative Technique and Distance in *The Dream of the Rood*', *Papers on Language & Literature* 6, pp. 293–301.

EKWALL, E. (1917), 'Ae. botl, bold, boðl in englischen ortsnamen', *AB*, XXVIII, pp. 82-91.

ELLIOTT, R. W. V. (1963), *Runes: An Introduction*, Second Edition (Manchester).

EVANS, A. C. (1986), *The Sutton Hoo Burial-Ship* (London).

FARINA, D. F. (1967), '*Wædum geweorðod* in *The Dream of the Rood*', *N & Q*, CCXII, pp. 4-6.

FARRELL, R. T. (1978), ed., *Bede and Anglo-Saxon England* (British Archaeological Reports, British Series 46).

FARRELL, R. T. (1986), 'Reflections of the Iconography of the Ruthwell and Bewcastle Crosses' in **SZARMARCH** (1986), pp. 357-76.

FARRELL, R. T. (1987), 'The Archer and Associated Figures on the Ruthwell Cross - a Reconsideration' in *Sources of Anglo-Saxon England: Papers in Honour of the 1300th Anniversary of the Birth of Bede, Given at Cornell University in 1973 and 1974*, ed. R. T. Farrell (British Archaeological Reports, 46), Oxford, pp. 96-117.

FERGUSON, E. (1997; repr. 1999), ed., *Encyclopedia of Early Christianity*, Second Edition (New York & London).

FINNEGAN, R. E. (1981), 'The *lifes weg rihtne* and *The Dream of the Rood*', *Revue de l'Université d'Ottawa*, LI, pp. 236-46.

FINNEGAN, R. E. (1983), 'The Gospel of Nicodemus and *The Dream of the Rood*', *NM*, LXXXIV, pp. 338-43.

FISHER, D. J. V. (1992), *The Anglo-Saxon Age: c 400 – 1042* (New York).

FLEMING, J. V. (1966), '*The Dream of the Rood* and Anglo-Saxon Monasticism', *Traditio*, 22, pp. 43–72.

FRANTZEN, A. J. (1986), *King Ælfred* (Boston).

FRERE, W. H. (1906), *The Principles of Religious Ceremonial* (London).

FULK, R. D. (1992), *A History of Old English Meter* (New York).

GARDE, J. N. (1991), *Old English Poetry in Medieval Christian Perspective* (Cambridge).

GARDNER, H. (1971; repr. 1983), *Religion and Literature* (Oxford).

GATCH, M. McC. (1977), *Preaching and Theology in Anglo-Saxon England* (Toronto).

GLASSCOE, M. (1987), ed., *The Medieval Mystical Tradition in England: Exeter Symposium IV* (Cambridge).

GODDEN, M. & **LAPIDGE**, M. (1991), eds., *The Cambridge Companion to Old English Literature* (Cambridge).

GRABAR, A. (1968), *Christian Iconography, A Study of Its Origins* (New York).

GRAYBILL, R. V. (1984), '*The Dream of the Rood*: Apotheosis of Anglo-Saxon Paradox' in **BOSSE**, et al. (1984), pp. 1-12.

GREENFIELD, S. B., & **CALDER***, D. G. (1986), *A New Critical History of Old English Literature with a Survey of the Anglo-Saxon Background by Michael Lapidge* (New York & London).

GRUBMÜLLER, K., et al. (1984), eds., *Geistliche Denkformen in der Literatur des Mittelalters* (Munich).

HALSALL, M. (1969), 'Vercelli and the Vercelli Book', *PMLA*, LXXXIV, pp. 1545-50.

HANEY, K. E. (1985), 'The Christ and the Beasts Panel on the Ruthwell Cross', *ASE*, XIV, pp. 215-31.

HAWKES, J., & **MILLS**, S. (1999), eds., *Northumbria's Golden Age* (Stroud, Gloucestershire).

HEDBERG, J. (1945), *The Syncope of the Old English Present Endings* (Lund).

HELDER, W. (1975), 'The *Engel Dryhtnes* in the *Dream of the Rood*', *MP*, LXXIII, pp. 148-50.

HENDERSON, G. (1985), 'The John the Baptist Panel on the Ruthwell Cross', *Gesta*, XXIV (no.1), pp.1-12.

HENDERSON, W. G. (1882), *Processionale ad usum Sarum* (London).

HENSEN, A. (1925), 'Het Egmonder Kruis', *Het Gildeboek*, VIII, pp. 92-7.

HERBEN, S. J. (1935), 'The Vercelli Book: A New Hypothesis', *Speculum*, X, pp. 91-4.

HERMANN, J. P. (1978), 'The Dream of the Rood, 19A: earmra ærgewin', *ELN*, XV, pp. 241-4.

HEWISON, J. K. (1914), *The Runic Roods of Ruthwell and Bewcastle* (Glasgow).

HIEATT, C. (1969), 'A New Theory of the Triple Rhythm in the Hypermetric Lines of Old English Verse', *MP*, LXVII, pp. 1-8.

HIEATT, C. (1971), 'Dream Frame and Verbal Echo in *The Dream of the Rood*', *NM*, 72, pp. 251–63.

HILL, D. (1981), ed., *An Atlas of Anglo-Saxon England* (Oxford).

HODGKIN, R. H. (1952), *A History of the Anglo-Saxons*, Third Edition (Cambridge).

HOLDSWORTH, C. (1982), 'Frames: Time Level and Variation in *The Dream of the Rood*', *Neophilologus*, LXVI, pp. 622-8.

HOLLOWAY, J. B. (1984), 'The Dream of the Rood and Liturgical Drama', *Comparative Drama*, XVIII, pp. 19-37.

HORGAN, A. D. (1978), '*The Dream of the Rood* and Christian Tradition', *NM*, LXXIX, pp. 11-20.

HORGAN, A. D. (1982), 'The Dream of the Rood and a Homily for Palm Sunday', *N & Q*, XXIX, pp. 388-91.

HOWLETT, D. R. (1974a), 'Three Forms of the Ruthwell Text in *The Dream of the Rood*', *English Studies*, LV, pp. 1-5.

HOWLETT, D. R. (1974b), 'Two Panels on the Ruthwell Cross', *Journal of the Warburg and Courtauld Insitutes*, XXXVII, pp. 333-6.

HOWLETT, D. R. (1976a), 'A Reconstruction of the Ruthwell Crucifixion Poem', *Studia Neophilologica*, XLVIII, pp. 54-8.

HOWLETT, D. R. (1976b), 'The Structure of the Dream of the Rood', *Studia Neophilologica*, XLVIII, pp. 301-6.

HOWLETT, D. R. (1978), 'Two Notes on *The Dream of the Rood*', *SN*, 50, pp. 167-73.

HOWLETT, D. R. (1992), 'Inscriptions and Design of the Ruthwell Cross' in **CASSIDY** (1992), pp. 71-94.

HOWORTH, H. H. (1914), 'The Great Crosses of the Seventh Century in Northern England', *Archaeological Journal*, LXXI, pp. 45-64.

HUNTER BLAIR, P. (1962; repr. 1977), *An Introduction to Anglo-Saxon England*, Second Edition (Cambridge).

HUNTER BLAIR, P. (1970; repr. 1990), *The World of Bede* (Cambridge).

HUPPÉ, B. F. (1970), 'The Dream of the Rood' in *The Web of Words*, (Albany), pp. 64-112.

IRVING, E. B. (1986), 'Crucifixion Witnessed, or Dramatic Interaction in *The Dream of the Rood*' in **BROWN, CRAMPTON, & ROBINSON** (1986), pp. 101–14.

ISAACS, N. D. (1968), 'Progressive Identifications: The Structural Principles of *The Dream of the Rood*', *Structural Principles in Old English Poetry* (Knoxville), pp. 3-18.

JACKSON, K. H. (1969), *The Goddodin: the Oldest Scottish Poem* (Edinburgh).

JARDINE GRISBROOKE, W. (1972; repr. 1978), 'Presanctified Mass' in **DAVIES** (1972; repr. 1978), pp. 322-3.

JONES, D. (1976), *Your Book of Anglo-Saxon England* (London).

JONES, G. (1968; repr. 1990), *A History of the Vikings* (Oxford).

JORDAN, R. (1906), *Eigentümlichkeiten des anglischen Wortschatzes* (Heidelberg).

KANNENGIESSER, C. & **BRIGHT**, P. (1996), *A Handbook of Patristic Exegesis* (Leiden).

KANTOROWICZ, E. H. (1960), 'The Archer in the Ruthwell Cross', *Art Bulletin*, XLII, pp. 57-9. Reprinted in *Selected Studies* (1965) New York, pp. 95-9.

KARKOV, C. E., **RYAN**, M., & **FARRELL**, T. F. (1997), eds., *The Insular Tradition* (Albany, New York).

KELLER, W. (1938), 'Zur Chronologie der ae. Runen', *Anglia*, LXII, pp. 24-38.

KELLY, J. N. D. (1964), ed., *The Athanasian Creed* (London).

KEMBLE, J. M. (1840), 'On Anglo-Saxon Runes', *Archaeologia*, XXVIII, pp. 327-72.

KEMBLE, J. M. (1844), 'Additional Observations on the Runic Obelisk at Ruthwell; the Poem of *The Dream of the Holy Rood*; . . .', *Archaeologia*, XXX, pp. 31-46.

KESSLER, H. L., & **SIMPSON**, M. S. (1985), eds., *Studies in the History of Art: Pictorial Narrative in Antiquity and the Middle Ages* (Washington, DC).

KESSLER, H. L. (1985), 'Pictorial Narrative and Church Mission in Sixth-Century Gaul' in **KESSLER & SIMPSON** (1985), pp. 75-91.

KEYNES, S., & **LAPIDGE**, M. (1983), ed., *Alfred the Great: Asser's Life of King Alfred and Other Contemporary Sources* (New York).

KILPIÖ, M. (1987), 'Hrabanus' *De Laudibus Sanctae Crucis* and *The Dream of the Rood*', *Neophilologica Fennica*, XLV, pp. 177-91.

KINTGEN, E. R. (1974), 'Echoic Repetitions in Old English Poetry, especially *The Dream of the Rood*', *NM*, 75, pp. 202–23.

KIRBY, D. P. (1992), *The Earliest English Kings* (London).

KIRBY, I. J. (1979), 'The Dream of the Rood: a Dilemma of Super-heroic Dimensions', *Etudes Lettres*, 4S, II, pp. 3-7.

KITZINGER, E. (1936), 'Anglo-Saxon Vine-Scroll Ornament', *Antiquity*, X, pp. 61-71.

KITZINGER, E. (1954), 'The Cult of Images in the Age before Iconoclasm', *Dumbarton Oaks Papers* 8, pp. 83-150. [Repr. (1976) in *The Art of Byzantium and the Medieval West: Selected Studies by Ernst Kitzinger*, edited by W. E. Kleinbauer, pp. 90-156.]

KLINCK, A. L. (1982), 'Christ as Soldier and Servant in *The Dream of the Rood*' *Florilegium*, IV, pp. 109-16.

KNOWLES, D. (1963), *The Monastic Order in Britain*, Second Edition (Cambridge).

KOCH, W. (1990), ed., *Epigraphik 1988. Fachtagung für mittelalterliche und neuzeitliche Epigraphik, Graz, 10-14 Mai 1988,*Österreichische Akademie der Wissenschaften, philosophisch-historische Klass, Denkschriften, Bd.213, (Vienna).

LAGORIO, V. M. (1986), ed., *Mysticism: Medieval & Modern* (Salzburg).

LAING, L., & **LAING**, J. (1979), *Anglo-Saxon England* (London).

LASS, R. (1994), *Old English: A Historical Linguistic Companion* (Cambridge).

LAWRENCE, C. H. (1984; repr. 1989), *Medieval Monasticism: Forms of Religious Life in Western Europe in the Middle Ages* (London & New York).

LEE, A. A. (1975), 'Towards a Critique of *The Dream of the Rood*' in **NICHOLSON & FRESE** (1975), pp. 163-91.

LEE, N. A. (1972), 'The Unity of the *The Dream of the Rood*', *Neophil*, 56, pp. 469–86.

LEHMANN, W. P., & **DAILEY**, V. F. (1960), *The Alliterations of the 'Christ', 'Guthlac', 'Elene', 'Juliana', 'The Fates of the Apostles', 'Dream of the Rood'* (Austin).

LEITER, L. H. (1967), '*The Dream of the Rood*: Patterns of Transformation' in **CREED** (1967), pp. 93-127.

LENDINARA, P. (1991), 'The World of Anglo-Saxon Learning' in **GODDEN & LAPIDGE** (1991), pp. 264-81.

LENTZNER, K. (1890), *Das Kreuz bei den Angelsachsen; gemeinverständliche aufzeichnungen* (Leipzig).

LESTER, G. A. (1976), *The Anglo-Saxons: How They Lived and Worked* (London & Vancouver).

LOGEMAN, H. (1891), *L'Inscription Anglo-Saxonne du Reliquaire de la Vraie Croix au Trésor de l'Église des SS. Michel-et-Gudule à Bruxelles* (Mémoires Couronnés . . . Publiés par l'Académie Royale de Belgique, Vol. XLV, Brussels).

LOWDEN, J. (1997), *Early Christian and Byzantine Art* (London).

LOYN, H. R. (1977), *The Vikings in Britain* (New York).

MacLEAN, D. (1992), 'The Date of the Ruthwell Cross' in **CASSIDY** (1992), pp. 49-70.

MacMULLEN, R. (1984), *Christianizing the Roman Empire AD 100-400* (New Haven).

MacNIOCAILL, G., & **WALLACE**, P. F. (1988), eds., *Keimelia: Studies in Medieval Archaeology in Memory of Tom Delaney* (Galway).

McENTIRE, S. (1986), 'The Devotional Context of the Cross before A.D. 1000' in **SZARMACH** (1986), pp. 345-56.

MACRAE-GIBSON, O. D. (1969), 'Christ the Victor-Vanquished in *The Dream of the Rood*', *NM*, 70, pp. 667–72.

MAHLER, A. E. (1978), '*Lignum Domini* and the Opening Vision of *The Dream of the Rood*: a Viable Hypothesis?', *Speculum*, LIII, pp. 441-59.

MARQUARDT, H. (1961), *Die Runeninschriften der Britischen Inseln; Bibliographie der Runeninschriften nach Fundorten*, I (Göttingen).

MARSH*, H. (1987), *Dark Age Britain: Sources of History* (New York).

MASTRO, M. L. Del (1976), '*The Dream of the Rood* and the *Militia Christi*: Perspective in paradox', *American Benedictine Review*, XXVII, pp. 171-86.

MAYR-HARTING, H. (1991), *The Coming of Christianity to Anglo-Saxon England*, Third Edition (London).

MERCIER, E. (1964), 'The Ruthwell and Bewcastle Crosses', *Antiquity*, XXXVIII, pp. 268-76.

MEYVAERT, P. (1982), 'An Apocalypse Panel on the Ruthwell Cross', *Medieval and Renaissance Studies*, IX, pp. 3-32.

MEYVAERT, P. (1992), 'A New Perspective on the Ruthwell Cross: Ecclesia and Vita Monastica' in **CASSIDY** (1992), pp. 95-166.

MITCHELL, B. (1995), *An Invitation to Old English & Anglo-Saxon England* (Oxford).

MITCHELL, B., & **ROBINSON**, F. C. (1992; repr. 1994), *A Guide to Old English*, Fifth Edition (Oxford).

MITCHELL, W. J. T. (1987), *Iconography: Image, Text, Ideology* (Chicago & London).

MUIR, P. M. (1905), 'The Ruthwell Cross', *Trans. Scottish Ecclesiological Society*, I, pp. 135-40.

NAPIERKOWSKI, T. J. (1978), 'A Dream of the Cross', *Concerning Poetry*, XI, pp. 3-12.

NETZER, N. (1994), *Cultural Interplay in the Eighth Century: The Trier Gospels and the Making of a Scriptorium at Echternach* (Cambridge).

NEUMAN DE VEGVAR, C. (1987), *The Northumbrian Renaissance: A Study in the Transmission of Style* (London & Toronto).

NICHOLSON, L. E. & **FRESE**, D. W. (1975), eds., *Anglo-Saxon Poetry: Essays in Appreciation* (Notre Dame).

NORMAN, F. (1936), Review of: H. Bütow (1935), Das altenglische 'Traumgesicht vom Kreuz', in *Beiblatt* zur *Anglia. Mitteilungen über englische Sprache und Literatur und über englischen Unterricht* XLVII, pp. 6-10.

Ó CARRAGÁIN, É. (1975), *The Vercelli Book as an Ascetic Florilegium* (Unpublished Thesis, Queen's University, Belfast).

Ó CARRAGÁIN, É. (1978), 'Liturgical Movements Associated with Pope Sergius and the Iconography of the Ruthwell and Bewcastle Crosses', in **FARRELL** (1978), pp. 131-47.

Ó CARRAGÁIN, É. (1982), 'Crucifixion as Annunciation: the Relation of *The Dream of the Rood* to the Liturgy Reconsidered', *English Studies*, LXIII, pp. 487-505.

Ó CARRAGÁIN, É. (1983), '*Vidi Aquam*: the Liturgical Background to *The Dream of the Rood* 20a: *swætan on þa swiðran healfe*', *N & Q*, CCXXVIII, pp. 8-15.

Ó CARRAGÁIN, É. (1986), 'Christ over the Beasts and the *Agnus Dei*: Two Multivalent Panels on the Ruthwell and Bewcastle Crosses' in **SZARMARCH** (1986), pp. 376-403.

Ó CARRAGÁIN, É. (1987a), 'A Liturgical Interpretation of the Bewcastle Cross' in **STOKES & BURTON** (1987), pp. 15-42.

Ó CARRAGÁIN, É. (1987b), 'The Ruthwell Cross and Irish High Crosses: Some Points of Comparison and Contrast' in **RYAN** (1987), pp. 118-28.

Ó CARRAGÁIN, É. (1987-88), 'The Ruthwell Crucifixion Poem in Its Iconographic and Liturgical Contexts', *Peritia. Journal of the Medieval Academy of Ireland*, VI-VII, pp. 1-71.

Ó CARRAGÁIN, É. (1988), 'The Meeting of Saint Paul and Saint Anthony: Visual and Literary Uses of a Eucharistic Motif' in **MacNIOCAILL & WALLACE** (1988), pp. 1-58.

Ó CARRAGÁIN, É. (1992), 'Seeing, Reading, Singing the Ruthwell Cross: Vernacular Poetry, Old Roman Liturgy, Implied Audience' in *Medieval Europe 1992, Pre-published Papers* VII, *Art and Symbolism*, pp. 91-6.

Ó CARRAGÁIN, É. (1994), '*Traditio Evangeliorum* and *Sustentatio*: The Relevance of Liturgical Ceremonies to the Book of Kells' in **O'MAHONY** (1994), pp. 398-436.

Ó CARRAGÁIN, É. (1995), 'Rome Pilgrimage, Roman Liturgy and the Ruthwell Cross', *Akten des XII. internationalen Kongresses für christliche Archäologie, Bonn, 22. Bis 28. September 1991* (Jahrbuch für Antike und Christentum, Ergänzungsband, 20, Parts 1 and 2), 2 Vols. (Münster), Vol. II, pp. 630-9.

Ó CARRAGÁIN, É. (1999), 'Rome, Ruthwell, Vercelli: *The Dream of the Rood* and the Italian Connection' in **DOLCETTI CORAZZA** (1999), pp. 59-100.

Ó CARRAGÁIN, É. (1999), 'The Necessary Distance: *Imitatio Romae* and the Ruthwell Cross' in **HAWKES & MILLS** (1999), pp. 191-203.

OKASHA, E. (1971), *Hand-List of Anglo-Saxon Non-Runic Inscriptions* (Cambridge).

OKASHA, E. (1983), 'A Supplement to Hand-List of Anglo-Saxon Runic Inscriptions', *ASE*, XI, pp. 83-118.

OKASHA, E. (1990), 'Vernacular or Latin? The languages of Insular Inscriptions, AD 500-1100' in **KOCH** (1990), pp. 139-147.

OKASHA, E. (1992), 'Literacy in Anglo-Saxon England: the Evidence from Inscriptions', *Medieval Europe 1992, Prepublished Papers VII, Art and Symbolism* (York).

O'LOUGHLIN, J. L. N. (1931), 'The Dream of the Rood', *Times Literary Supplement*, XXX, p. 648.

O'MAHONY, F. (1994), ed., *The Book of Kells: Proceedings of a Conference at Trinity College Dublin, 6-9 September 1992.* (Aldershot, UK; Vermont, USA).

OMAN, C. (1993), *A History of England before the Norman Conquest* (London).

ORTON, P. (1980), 'The Technique of Subject-Personification in *The Dream of the Rood* and a Comparison with the Old English Riddles', *Leeds Studies in English*, n.s. 11, pp. 1–18.

OWEN, G. R. (1981), *Rites and Religions of the Anglo-Saxons* (Newton Abbot, Devon).

PAGE, R. I. (1959a), 'Language and Dating in OE Inscriptions', *Anglia. Zeitschrift für englische Philologie*, LXXVII, pp. 385-406.

PAGE, R. I. (1959b), 'An Early Drawing of the Ruthwell Cross', *Medieval Archaeology*, iii, pp. 285-88.

PAGE, R. I. (1962), 'The Use of Double Runes in Old English Inscriptions', *Journal of English and German Philology*, LXI (no. 4), pp. 897-907.

PAGE, R. I. (1970), *Life in Anglo-Saxon England* (London).

PAGE, R. I. (1973), *An Introduction to English Runes* (London).

PAGE, R. I. (1987), *Runes* (London).

PAGE, R. I. (1990), 'Dating Old English Inscriptions: The Limits of Inference' in **ADAMSON, LAW, VINCENT, & WRIGHT** (1990), pp. 357-77.

PALGRAVE, F. (1989), *History of the Anglo-Saxons* (New York).

PASTERNACK, C. B. (1984), 'Stylistic Disjunctions in *The Dream of the Rood*', *ASE*, XIII, pp. 167-86.

PATCH, H. R. (1919), 'Liturgical Influence in *The Dream of the Rood*', *PMLA*, 34, pp. 233–57.

PATTEN, F. H. (1968), 'Structure and Meaning in *The Dream of the Rood*', *ES*, 49, pp. 385–401.

PAYNE, R. C. (1976), 'Convention and Originality in the Vision Framework of *The Dream of the Rood*' *MP*, 73, pp. 329–41.

PETERSON, P. W. (1953), 'Dialect Grouping in the Unpublished Vercelli Homilies', *Studies in Philology*, 1, pp. 559-65.

PEZZINI, D. (1972), 'Teologia e poesia: la sintesi del poema anglosassone *Sogno della Croce*' *Rendiconti del' Istituto Lombardo*, CVI, pp. 268-86.

PICKFORD, T. E. (1976), '*Holmwudu* in *The Dream of the Rood*', *NM*, LXXVII, pp. 561-4.

POLLINGTON, S. (1989), *The Warrior's Way: England in the Viking Age* (London).

POPE, J. C. (1942; rev. 1966), *The Rhythm of Beowulf* (Yale).

RAW, B. C. (1967), 'The Archer, the Eagle and the Lamb', *Journal of the Warburg and Courtauld Institutes*, XXX, pp. 391-4.

RAW, B. C. (1970), '*The Dream of the Rood* and Its Connections with Early Christian Art', *MÆ*, 39, pp. 239–56.

RAW, B. C. (1990), *Anglo-Saxon Crucifixion Iconography and the Art of the Monastic Revival*, Cambridge Studies in Anglo-Saxon England, 1 (Cambridge).

RAW, B. C. (1997), *Trinity and Incarnation in Anglo-Saxon Art and Thought*, Cambridge Studies in Anglo-Saxon England, 21 (Cambridge).

RENOIR, A. (1976), 'Oral Theme and Written Texts', *NM*, LXXVII, pp. 337-46.

RICCI, A. (1929), 'The Chronology of Anglo-Saxon Poetry', *RES*, V, pp. 257-66.

RICHÉ, P. (1976), *Education and Culture in the Barbarian West, Sixth through Eighth*, trans. J. J. Contreni (Columbia, SC).

RISSANEN, M. (1967), 'Two Notes on Old English Poetic Texts', *NM*, LXVIII, pp. 283-7.

RISSANEN, P. (1987), *The Message and the Structure of The Dream of the Rood* (Helsinki).

ROSS, A. S. C. (1933), 'The Linguistic Evidence for the Date of the Ruthwell Cross', *MLR*, XXVIII, pp. 145-55.

RUSSOM, G. (1987), *Old English Meter and Linguistic Theory* (Cambridge).

RYAN, M. (1987), ed., *Ireland and Insular Art: A.D. 500 - 1200* (Dublin).

RYDBERG, V. (1874; repr. 1899), 'Skalden Kadmon och Ruthwell-korset' *Göteborgs Handels- och Sjöfartstidning*, 24 September 1874, 3. Reprinted in *Skrifter af Viktor Rydberg*, XIV (Stockholm), pp. 516-23.

SARRAZIN, G. (1913), *Von Kädmon bis Kynewulf* (Berlin).

SAVAGE, A. (1986), 'Mystical and Evangelical in *The Dream of the Rood*: the Private and the Public' in **LAGORIO** (1986), pp. 4-11.

SAVAGE, A. (1987), 'The Place of Old English Poetry in the English Meditative Tradition' in **GLASSCOE** (1987), pp. 91-110.

SAXL, F. (1943; repr. 1945), 'The Ruthwell Cross', *Journal of the Warburg and Courtauld Institutes*, VI, pp. 1-19. Reprinted in *England and the Mediterranean Tradition*, Warburg & Courtauld Institutes, University of London (London), pp. 1-19.

SCHAAR, C. (1949), *Critical Studies in the Cynewulf Group* (Lund).

SCHAPIRO, M. (1944), 'The Religious Meaning of the Ruthwell Cross', *Art Bulletin*, XXVI, pp. 232-45.

SCHAPIRO, M. (1963), 'The Bowman and the Bird on the Ruthwell Cross and other Works', *Art Bulletin*, XLV, pp. 351-5.

SCHILLER, G. (1971), *Iconography of Christian Art*, Vol. I (London).

SCHLAUCH, M. (1940), '*The Dream of the Rood* as Prosopopoeia', *Essays and Studies in Honor of Carleton Brown* (New York), pp. 23-34.

SCHMITZ, T. (1910), 'Die Sechstakter in der altenglischen Dichtung', *Anglia*, XXXIII, pp. 58-63.

SCHÜCKING, L. L. (1908), 'Das angelsächsische Totenklagelied', *ES*, XXXIX, pp. 1-13.

SCHWAB, U. (1978), '*Das Traumgesicht vom Kreuzesbaum*: ein ikonologischer Interpretationsansatz zu dem ags. *Dream of the Rood*', in **SCHWAB & STUTZ** (1978), pp. 131-92.

SCHWAB, U., & STUTZ, E. (1978), eds., *Philologische Studien: Gedenkschrift für Richard Kienast* (Heidelberg).

SCHWAB, U. (1984), 'Exegetische und homiletische Stilformen in *Dream of the Rood*', in K. **GRUBMÜLLER** et al., (1984), pp. 101-30.

SCRAGG, D. G. (1968), '*Hwæt/þæt* in *The Dream of the Rood*, Line 2', *N & Q*, CCXIII, pp. 166-8.

SCRAGG, D. G. (1973), 'The Compilation of the Vercelli Book', *ASE*, II, pp. 189-207.

SHEPHERD, G. (1966), 'Scriptural Poetry' in **STANLEY** (1966), pp. 1-36.

SIEVERS, E. (1893), *Altgermanische Metrik* (Halle).

SIEVERS, E. (1895), 'Zur Rhythmik des germanischen Alliterations-verses', *Beiträge zur Geschichte der deutschen Sprache und Literatur*, edited by H. Paul & W. Braune, pp. 464-5.

SIMONETTI, M. (1994), *Biblical Interpretation in the Early Church: An Historical Introduction to Patristic Exegesis* (Edinburgh).

SIMS-WILLIAMS, P. (1990), *Religion and Literature in Western England, 600-800* (Cambridge).

SISAM, K. (1913), 'Epenthesis in the Consonant Groups *sl, sn*', *Archiv.*, CXXXI, pp. 305-10.

SISAM, K. (1946; repr. 1953), 'Notes on Old English Poetry', *RES*, XXII, pp. 257-68. Reprinted in **SISAM** (1953), pp. 29-44.

SISAM, K. (1953), 'Dialect Origins of the Earlier Old English Verse' in **SISAM** (1953), pp. 119-39.

SISAM, K. (1953), *Studies in the History of Old English Literature* (Oxford).

SKEMP, A. R. (1906-7), 'The Transformation of Scriptural Story, Motive, and Conjecture in Anglo-Saxon Poetry', *MP*, IV, pp. 423-70.

SMITH, A. H. (1933; repr. 1968), ed., *Three Northumbrian Poems* (London).

SMITH, A. H. (1956), *English Place-Name Elements* (Cambridge).

SMITH, J. (1975), 'The Garments that Honour the Cross in *The Dream of the Rood*', *ASE*, IV, pp. 29-35.

SOUTHERN, R. W. (1953; repr. 1959), *The Making of The Middle Ages* (London).

STANLEY, E. G. (1966), ed., *Continuations and Beginnings* (London).

STANLEY, E. G. (1975), *The Search for Anglo-Saxon Paganism* (Cambridge & Totowa).

STANLEY, E. G. (1987), 'The Ruthwell Cross Inscription: Some linguistic and Literary Implications of Paul Meyvaert's Paper 'An Apocalypse Panel on the Ruthwell Cross'' in **STANLEY** (1987), pp. 384-99.

STANLEY*, E. G. (1987), ed., *A Collection of Papers with Emphasis on Old English Literature*, Publications of the Dictionary of Old English 3, (Toronto & Leiden).

STENTON, F. (1971; repr. 1989), *Anglo-Saxon England*, Third Edition (Oxford).

STEVENS, W. O. (1904), *The Cross in the Life and Literature of Anglo-Saxons* (New York).

STEVICK, R. D. (1967), 'The Meter of *The Dream of the Rood*', *NM*, LXVIII, pp. 149-68.

STOKES, M., & **BURTON**, T. L. (1987), eds., *Medieval Literature and Antiquities. Studies in Honor of Basil Cottle* (Cambridge).

SZARMACH, P. E. (1986), ed., *Sources of Anglo-Saxon Culture* (Toronto).

SZARMACH, P. E. (1996), ed., *Holy Men and Holy Women: Old English Prose Saints' Lives and Their Contexts* (New York).

SZÖVERFFY, J. (1966), ' "*Crux Fidelis . . .* " Prolegomena to a History of the Holy Cross Hymns', *Traditio*, 22, pp. 1-41.

SWANTON, M. J. (1969), 'Ambiguity and Anticipation in *The Dream of the Rood*', *NM*, LXX, pp. 407-25.

TALBOT RICE, D. (1963; repr. 1997), *Art of the Byzantine Era* (London)

TALLEY, T. (1986), *The Origins of the Liturgical Year* (New York).

TATE, G. S. (1978), 'Chiasmus as Metaphor: the *Figura Crucis* Tradition and *The Dream of the Rood*', *NM*, LXXIX, pp. 114-25.

TAYLOR, P. B. (1974), 'Text and Texture of *The Dream of the Rood*' *NM*, LXXV, pp. 193-201.

TEMPLE, E. (1976), *Anglo-Saxon Manuscripts, 900-1066.* Survey of Manuscripts Illuminated in the British Isles, 2 (London).

TRAUTMANN, M. (1898), *Kynewulf, der Bischof und Dichter* (Bonn).

TRIPP, R. P. (1971), 'The Dream of the Rood: 9b and its Context', *MP*, LXIX, pp. 136-7.

WALLACE, A. D., & **ROSS**, W. O. (1958), eds., *Studies in Honor of John Wilcox* (Detroit).

WEBSTER, L., & **BLACKHOUSE**, J. (1991), eds., *The Making of England. Anglo-Saxon Art and Culture, AD 600-900* (London & Toronto).

WEIGHTMAN, J. (1907), *The Language and the Dialect of the Later Old English Poetry* (Liverpool).

WEITZMANN, K. (1978), *The Icon* (New York).

WHITELOCK, D. (1974; repr. 1979) *The Beginnings of English Society*, Second Edition (Harmondsworth).

WHITLOCK, R. (1977), *Warrior Kings of Saxon England* (Bradford-on-Avon, Wilts.).

WHITTOCK, M. J. (1986), *The Origins of England: 410 – 600* (New York).

WHITMAN, F. H. (1975), '*The Dream of the Rood*, 101a', *The Explicator*, XXXIII, p. 70.

WHITMAN, F. H. (1993), *A Comparative Study of Old English Metre* (Toronto).

WILLETT, F. (1957), 'The Ruthwell and Bewcastle Crosses', *Memoirs of the Manchester Literary and Philosophical Society*, XCVIII, pp. 94-136.

WILLIAMS, P. (1938), *I am Canute* (London).

WILLIAMS, P. (1951), *Ælfred the King* (London).

WILSON, D. M. (1980), *The Northern World: The History and Heritage of Northern Europe, AD 400-1000* (London).

WILSON, D. M. (1981), *The Anglo-Saxons*, Third Edition (Middlesex).

WOLF, C. J. (1970), 'Christ as Hero in *The Dream of the Rood*', *NM*, LXXI, pp. 202–10.

WOOD, M. (1987), *In Search of the Dark Ages* (New York).

WOOLF, R. (1958), 'Doctrinal Influences in *The Dream of the Rood*', *MÆ*, 27, No. 3, pp. 137–53.

WORMALD, F. (1945), 'Decorated Initials in English MSS from AD 900 to 1100', *Archaeologia*, XCI, pp. 120-43.

WRENN, C. L. (1943; repr. 1967), 'The Value of Spelling as Evidence' *Trans. Philological Society*, pp. 14-39. Reprinted in *Word and Symbol; Studies in English Language* (London), pp. 129-49.

WÜLCKER, R. P. (1878), 'Ueber den Dichter Cynewulf', *Anglia*, I, pp. 483-507.

ZUPITZA, J. (1891), 'Review of Logeman, L'Inscription Anglo-Saxonne', *Archiv.* LXXXVII, p. 462.

Glossary

This glossary lists all grammatical word-forms in the Old English poetic texts which occur in this edition. Those of the Ruthwell Cross and the Brussels Cross Inscription are intercalated with corresponding Vercelli Codex forms (denoted by line number) and are indicated in parenthesis by the abbreviations RC (with line numbers according to the edited text on p. 38) and BCI (with no line numbers). The order of words is alphabetical: æ follows ad-, words prefixed with ge- follow geara, and ð & þ are treated as one letter and follow t. The gender of nouns are abbreviated to *m.*, *f.*, and *n.* (noun being implied). The numbers after *sv.* and *wv.* refer to the classes of strong and weak verbs in turn. Word definitions, the order, and declined forms within the Glossary are consonant with Swanton (1987; repr. 1992). All abbreviations used are expanded in the List of Abbreviations and Grammatical Terms (pp. x-xii).

ac *conj.* but 11, 43, 115, 119,132, (RC 4).

Adom *prop. name* Adam; *gen. sg.* **Adomes** 100.

æfentid *f.* evening-time; *acc. sg.* **æfentide** 68.

æfter *prep. w. dat.* after 65.

æghwylc *adj.* each, every; *f. nom. sg.* 120.

æghwylc *pron.* everyone; *m. acc. sg.* **æghwylcne (anra)** 86.

Ælfric *prop. name* Ælfric; *gen. sg.* **Ælfrices** (BCI).

ælmihtig *adj.* almighty; *m. nom. sg.* 39, 93, 98, 106, 153, 156, (RC **alme3ttig** 1); *m. acc. sg.* **ælmihtigne** 60.

ænig *pron.* any, anyone; *m. nom. sg.* 110, 117; *m. dat. sg. (neg.)* **nænigum** 47.

ær *adv.* before, formally 114, 118, 137, 145, 154; *comp.* **ærur** earlier 108; *sup.* **ærest** first 19.

ærgewin *n.* former struggle, strife; *acc. sg.* 19.

ærþan *conj.* before 88.

æt *prep. w. dat.* at 8, 63, (RC 15).

ætgædere *adv.* together 48, (RC **ætgadre** 7).

æðeling *m.* lord, prince; *dat. sg.* **æðelinge** 58.

Æþlmær *prop. name* Æthlmær; *nom. sg.* (BCI).

æþþilæ *adjvl. noun* noble ones; *nom. pl.* (RC 11).

afysan *wv.* 1 to impel, urge forward; *pp. m. nom. sg.* **afysed** 125.

agan *pret. pres. v.* to have, possess; *1 sg. pres. (neg.)* **nah** 131; *3 sg. pres.* **ah** 107.

aheawan *sv.* 7 to hew, cut down; *pp. m. nom. sg.* **aheawen** 29.

ahebban *sv.* 6 to raise, lift up (lift down, remove 61); *1 sg. pret.* **ahof** 44; *3 pl. pret.* **ahofon** 61.

alecgan *wv.* 1 to lay down; *3 pl. pret.* **aledon** 63, (RC **alegdun** 14).

an *adj.* one; *wk. m. nom. sg.* **ana** alone 123, 128; *m. dat. sg* **anum**. (RC 11); *gen. pl.* **anra** 86, 108; see **æghwylcne (anra)** and **(anra) gehwylc.**

anforht *adj.* very frightened, terrified; *m. nom. sg.* 117.

Anwealda *m.* sovereign, lord; *nom. sg.* 153.

aræran *wv.* 1 to rear, raise up; *pp. m. nom. sg.* **aræred** 44.

arisan *sv.* 1 to rise, arise; *3 sg. pret.* **aras** 101.

asettan *wv.* 1 to set, place; *3 pl. pret.* **asetton** 32; *3 sg. pres. subj.* **asette** 142.

astigan *sv.* 1 to mount, ascend; *3 sg. pret.* **astag** 103.

astyrian *wv.* 1 to move, remove; *pp. m. nom. sg.* **astyred** 30.

Aðelwold *prop. name* Athelwold; *nom. sg.*(BCI).

ba *adj.* both; *f. acc.* (RC 7).

bana *m.* slayer; *gen. sg.* **banan** 66.

beacen *n.* symbol, sign, standard; *nom. sg.* 6; *acc. sg.* 21; *dat. sg.*

beacne 83; *gen. pl.* **beacna** 118.

bealuware *m. collective nn.* dwellers in evil, evil men; *gen. sg.* **bealuwara** 79.

beam *m.* tree, part of a tree or ray of light; *nom. sg.* 97; *dat. sg.* **beame** 114, 122; *gen. pl.* **beama** 6.

bearn *n.* son, child; *nom. sg.* 83.

bedelfan *sv.* 3 to bury; *3 sg. pret.* **bedealf** 75.

bedrifan *sv.* 1 to cover, drench, soak; *pp. m. acc. sg.* **bedrifenne** 62.

begeotan *sv.* 2 to sprinkle, shed, pour out; *pp. n. nom. sg.* **begoten** 7, 49, (RC **bigoten** 8).

behealdan *sv.* 7 to behold, gaze on, watch over; *1 sg. pret.* **beheold** 25, 58, (RC **biheald** 11); *3 pl. pret.* **beheoldan** 9, 11, 64, (RC **bihealdun** 16).

beon see **wesan**.

beorg *m.* mound, hill; *acc. sg.* 32; *dat. sg.* **beorge** 50.

beorht *adj.* bright, shining; *wk. m. dat. sg.* **beorhtan** 66; *sup. n. acc. sg.* **beorhtost** 6.

beorn *m.* man, warrior; *nom sg.* 42; *nom. pl.* **beornas** 32, 66.

beran *sv.* 4 to bear, carry; *3 sg. pres.* **bereð** 118; *1 sg. pret.* **bær** (BCI); *3 pl. pret.* **bæron** 32.

berstan *sv.* 3 to burst, break 36.

besteman *wv.* 1 to make wet; *pp. m. n. nom. sg.* **bestemed** 22, 48, (BCI), (RC **bistemid** 7).

beswyllan *wv.* 1 to soak, drench; *pp. n. nom. sg.* **beswyled** 23.

bewindan *sv.* 3 to wrap, wind round; *pp. n. acc. sg.* **bewunden** 5.

bewreon *sv.* 1 to cover, clothe; *pp.* **bewrigen(e)** 17, 53.

bifian *wv.* 2 to tremble, shake 36; *1 sg. pret.* **bifode** 42; *pp.* **byfigynde** (BCI).

biter *adj.* bitter, painful; *m. gen. sg.* **biteres** 114.

bled *m.* glory, blessedness; *dat. pl.* **bledum** 149.

bleo *n.* colour; *dat. pl.* **bleom** 22.

blis *f.* gladness, pleasure, bliss; *nom. sg.* 139, 141; *dat. sg.* **blisse** 149, 153.

bilðe *adj.* joyful, glad; *n. dat. sg.* 122.

blod *n.* blood; *dat. sg.* **blode** 48, (BCI), (RC **blodæ** 7).

breost *n.* breast, heart; *dat. pl.* **breostum** 118.

broþor *m.* brother; *nom. sg.* **beroþor** (BCI).

brucan *sv.* 2 to enjoy, partake of 144.

bryne *m.* burning, hellfire; *acc. sg.* 149.

bugan *sv.* 2 to bend, bow down 36, (RC **buga** 4).

butu *adj.* both; *n. acc.* 48.

byrigan *wv.* 1 to taste; *3 sg. pret.* **byrigde** 101.

bysmerian *wv* 2 or 3 to mock, insult; *3 pl. pret.* **bysmeredon** 48, (RC **bismærædu** 7).

ceorfan *sv.* 3 to carve, cut out; *3 pl. pret.* **curfon** 66.

colian *wv.* 2 to cool, grow cold; *3 sg. pret.* **colode** 72.

Crist *prop. name* Christ; *nom. sg.* 56, (RC **Krist** 9); *dat. sg.* **Criste** 116.

cuman *sv.* 4 to come; *3 sg. pret.* **com** 151, **cwom** 155; *3 pl. pret.* **cwoman** 57, (RC **kwomu** 10); *pp. m. nom. sg.* **cumen** 80.

cweðan *sv.* 5 to say, declare 116; *3 sg. pres.* (*future sense*) **cwyð** 111.

cwiðan *wv.* 1 to lament, mourn; *3 pl. pret.* **cwiðdon** 56.

Cyning *m.* King; *acc. sg.*, 44, 133, (BCI), (RC **Kyninge** 5); *gen. sg.* **Cyninges** 56.

cynn *n.* kin, race; **wifa cynn** womankind *acc. sg.* 94.

cyst *f.* choice, choicest, best; *acc. sg.* 1.

dæg *m.* day; *gen. pl.* **daga** 136.

deað *m.* death; *acc. sg.* 101; *gen.*

sg. **deaðes** 113.

deman *wv. 1* (*w. dat.*) to judge 107.

deop *adj.* deep; *wk. m. dat. sg.*
deopan 75.

deorc *adj.* dark; *wk. m. dat. pl.*
deorcan 46.

dolg *n.* wound; *nom. pl.* 46.

dom *m.* judgement; *gen. sg.*
domes 107.

domdæg *m.* Doomsday, Judgement
Day; *dat. sg.* **domdæge** 105.

don *anom. v.* to do; *3 sg. pret.*
dyde 114.

dream *m.* joy, delight; *nom. sg.*
140; *gen. sg.* **dreames** 144; *dat.*
pl. **dreamum** 133.

Dryhten *m.* Lord; *nom. sg.* 101, 105;
voc. sg. 144; *acc. sg.* 64, (RC **Dryctin**
16); *gen. sg.* **Dryhtnes** 9, 35, 75, 113,
136, 140.

durran *pret. pres. v.* to dare; *1 sg.*
pret. **dorste** 35, 42, 45, 47, (RC
dorstæ 6).

eac *adv.* also 92.

ealdgewyrht *f. n.* old or former
action; *dat. pl.* **ealdgewyrhtum**
100.

ealdor *m.* prince, lord; *nom. sg.*
90.

eall *adj.* all; *n. nom. sg.* 6; *f. nom.*
sg. 12, **eal** 55, 82; *n. acc. sg.*
58, 94, (RC **al** 11); *m. nom. pl.*
ealle 9, 128; *m. acc. pl.* **ealle**
37, 74, 93, (RC **allæ** 3); *gen. pl.*
ealra in all 125; *m. dat. pl.*
eallum 154.

eall *adv.* all, completely 20, 48,
62.

earm *adj.* wretched; *m. nom. pl.*
earme 68; *as noun, m. gen. pl.*
earmra 19.

eaðmod *adj.* humble; *n. nom. sg.*
60.

eaxl *f.* shoulder; *dat. pl.* **eaxlum**
32.

eaxlegespann *n.* cross-beam, junc-
tion of the cross; *dat. sg.*
eaxlegespanne 9.

efstan *wv.* 1 to hurry, make haste
34.

eft *adv.* afterwards, again 68, 101,
103.

egesa *m.* awe, fear; *nom. sg.* 86.

egeslic *adj.* fearful, dreadful; *f.*
nom. sg. 74.

ellen *m.* strength, courage, zeal;
dat. sg. **elne** 34, 60, 123.

ende *m.* end, edge; *dat. sg.* 29.

engel *m.* angel; *acc. sg.* 9; *nom. pl.*
englas 106; *dat. pl.* **englum** 153.

eorðe *f.* earth, ground; *gen. sg.*
eorðan 37; *dat. sg.* 42, 74, 137,
145.

eorðweg *m.* earth, earthly way;
dat. sg. **eorðwege** 120.

eðel *m.* country, homeland; *nom.*
sg. 156.

fæger *adj.* fair, beautiful; *n. nom.*
sg. 73; *m. nom. pl.* **fægere** 8, 10;
wk. f. dat. sg. **fægran** 21.

fæste *adv.* firmly, securely 38,
43, (RC **fæstæ** 4).

fah *adj.* stained, guilty *or* brightly
coloured; *m. nom. sg.* 13.

fea *adv.* little 115.

feala *indecl. n. pron.* much, many
50, 125, 131.

feallan *sv.* 7 to fall 43.

feond *m.* fiend, foe, evil man;
nom. pl. **feondas** 30, 33; *acc. pl.*
38.

feorgbold *n.* body, the dwelling of
the spirit; *nom. sg.* 140.

feorran *adv.* from afar 57,
(RC **fearran** 10).

fif *adj.* five; *m. nom.* **fife** 8.

folc *n.* people; *nom. sg.* 140.

folde *f.* earth, ground; *gen. sg.*
foldan 8, 43; *dat. sg.* 132.

for *prep.* for, because of, for the
sake of, before, in front of; *w.*
dat. 21, 99, 111, 112, 113, 146;
w. acc. 93, (RC **fore** 3).

forgiefan *sv.* 5 to give, to grant; *3 sg.*
pret. **forgeaf** 147.

forht *adj.* afraid; *m. nom. sg.* 21.

forhtian *wv.* 2 to be afraid; *3 pl.*
pres. (*future sense*) **forhtiað** 115.

forlætan *sv.* 7 to leave; *3 pl. pret.*
forleton 61.

forð *adv.* forth, away 54, 132.

forþan *conj.* therefore 84.

forðgesceaft *f.* creation, that which is preordained; *acc. sg.* 10.

forðweg *m.* a going forth, departure; *dat. sg.* **forðwege** 125.

forwundian *wv.* 2 to wound badly; *pp. m. nom. sg.* **forwunded** 14, **forwundod** 62.

fracod *adjvl. noun* wicked, vile one; *gen. sg.* **fracodes** 10.

fram *prep. w. dat.* from, away from 69.

Frea *m.* Lord; *acc. sg.* **Frean** 33.

freond *m.* friend; *nom. sg.* 144; *nom pl.* **freondas** 76; *gen. pl.* **freonda** 132.

frinan *sv.* 3 to ask; *3 sg. pres.* (*future sense*) **frineð** 112.

fundian *wv.* 2 to come; *3 sg. pres.* **fundaþ** 103.

fus *adj.* hastening, eager, doomed; *n. acc. sg.* **fuse** 21; *as noun, m. nom. pl.* **fuse** 57, (RC **fusæ** 10).

fyll *m.* fall, death; *acc. sg.* 56.

fyllan *wv.* 1 to fell, cut down 73.

galan *sv.* 6 to sing 67.

gan *anom. v.* to go; *3 sg. pret.* **eode** 54.

gang *m.* flow; *dat. sg.* **gange** 23.

gast *m.* spirit, soul; *acc. sg.* 49, (RC **gastæ** 8); *nom. pl.* **gastas** 11; *gen. pl.* **gasta** 152.

gealga *m.* gallows; *nom. sg.* 10; *acc. sg.* **gealgan** 40, (RC **galgu** 2).

gealgtreow *n.* gallows-tree; *dat. sg.* **gealgtreowe** 146.

geara *adv.* long ago; **geara iu** very long ago 28.

gebidan *sv.* 1 to endure; *1 sg. pret.* **gebad** 125; *pp. m. nom. sg.* **gebiden** 50, 79.

gebiddan *sv.* 5 (*w. refl, dat.*) to pray, worship; *3 pl. pres.* **gebiddaþ** 83; *1 sg. pret.* **gebæd** 122.

gebringan *wv.* 1 to bring; *3 sg. pres. subj.* **gebringe** 139.

gedrefan *wv.* 1 to trouble, distress; *pp. nom. sg. m.* **gedrefed** 20, 59,

(RC **gidrœfid** 12).

geearnian *wv.* 2 to earn, gain, deserve; *3 sg. pres.* **geearnaþ** 109.

gefæstnian *wv.* 2 to fasten, make fast; *3 pl. pret.* **gefæstnodon** 33.

gefetian *wv.* 2 *or* 3 to fetch; *3 sg. pres. subj.* **gefetige** 138.

gefrinan *sv.* 3 to hear of; *3 pl. pret.* **gefrunon** 76.

gefyllan *wv.* 1 to fell, strike down 38.

gegyrwan *wv.* 1 to adorn; *pp. n. acc. sg.* **gegyred** 16, **gegyrwed** 23.

gehwylc *pron.* each, every; *m. inst. sg.* **gehwylce** 136; *m. dat. pl.* **gehwylcum** 108; see **anra (gehwylc)**.

gehyran *wv.* 1 to hear, understand 78; *1 sg. pret.* **gehyrde** 26.

gemætan *wv.* 1 (*impers. w. dat.*) to dream; *3 sg. pret.* **gemætte** 2.

gemunan *pret. pres. v.* to remember; *1 sg. pres.* **geman** 28.

geniman *sv.* 4 to take away, seize; *3 pl. pret.* **genaman** 30, **genamon** 60.

geniwian *wv.* 2 to renew, restore; *pp. m. nom. sg.* **geniwad** 148.

genog *adj.* enough, many; *m. nom. pl.* **genoge** 33.

geo *adv.* formally (BCI).

geong *adj.* young; *m. nom. sg.* 39.

gerihtan *wv.* 1 to direct; *pp. f. nom. sg.* **geriht** 131.

geryman *wv.* 1 to open, prepare, make way for; *1 sg. pret.* **gerymde** 89.

gesceaft *f.* creation; *nom. sg.* 12, 55, 82.

gesecan *wv.* 1 to reach (by seeking) 119.

geseon *sv.* 5 to see, behold; *1 sg. pret.* **geseah** 14, 21, 33, 36, 51; *1 sg. pret. subj.* **gesawe** 4.

gesettan *wv.* 1 to set, place; *3 pl. pret.* **gesetton** 67; *pp. n. nom. sg.* **geseted** 141.

gesiene *adj.* visible; *m. nom. pl.* 46.

gestandan *sv.* 6 to stand; *3 pl. pret.* **gestodon** 63, (RC **gistoddun** 15).

gestigan *sv.* 1 to mount, ascend 34, (RC **gistiga** 2); *3 sg. pret.* **gestah** 40.

gesyhð *n.* power, control; *acc. sg.* **gesyhðe** 96; *dat. sg.* 21, 41, 66.

geweald *n.* power, control; *acc. sg.* 107.

geweorðan *sv.* 3 to become; *pp. m. nom. sg.* **geworden** 87.

geweorðian *wv.* 2 to honour, adorn; *3 sg. pret.* **geweorðode** 90, 94; *pp. n. acc. sg.* **geweorðode** 15.

gewinn *n.* conflict struggle; *dat. sg.* **gewinne** 65.

gewitan *sv.* 1 to go depart; *3 sg. pret.* **gewat** 71; *3 pl. pret.* **gewiton** 133.

gewyrcan *wv.* 1 to make; *3 pl. pret.* **geworhton** 31.

gimm *m.* gem, jewel; *nom. pl.* **gimmas** 7, 16.

giwundian *wv.* 2 to wound; *pp.* (RC **giwundad** 13).

God *m.* God; *nom.* 39, 93, 98, 106, 156; *acc.* 51, 60; *gen.* **Godes** 83, 152.

god *adj.* good, great; *f. acc. sg.* **gode** 70; *sup. m. nom. sg.* **selesta** 27; *sup. n. acc. sg.* **selest** 118.

gold *n.* gold; *acc. sg.* 18; *dat. sg,* **golde** 7, 16, 77.

greotan *sv.* 2 to weep, to cry; *pp. m. nom. sg.* **greotende** 70,

guma *m.* man, collectively mankind; *gen. sg.* **guman** 49, 146, (RC 8).

gyrwan *wv.* 1 to dress, adorn; *3 pl. pret.* **gyredon** 77.

gyta *adv.* yet, still 28.

habban *wv.* 3 to have; *1 sg. pres.* **hæbbe** 50, 79; *3 sg. pret.* **hæfde** 49; *3 pl. pret.* **hæfdon** 16, 52.

hælan *wv.* 1 to heal, save 85.

hælda see **hyldan**.

Hælend *m.* Saviour; *gen. sg.* **Hælendes** 25.

hæleð *m.* man, hero; *nom. sg.* 39; *voc. sg.* 78, 95.

halga *m.* holy one, saint; *dat pl.* **halgum** 143, 154.

halig *adj.* holy; *m. nom. pl.* **halige** 11.

ham *m.* home, dwelling; *acc. sg.* 148.

hand *f.* hand; *dat. sg.* **handa** 59, (RC 12).

hatan *sv.* 7 to command; *1 sg. pres.* **hate** 95; *3 pl. pret.* **heton** 31.

he, hit *pron.* he, it; *m. nom. sg.* 34, 40, etc., (RC 8, 16); *n. nom. sg.* **hit** 19, 22, 26, 97; *m. acc. sg.* **hine** 11, 39, 61, 64, (RC **hinæ** 1, 14, 16); *m. gen. sg.* **his** 49, 63, 92, 102, 106, 156, (RC 8, 15), (BCI **hys**); *m. gen. pl.* **hyra** (BCI); *m. n. dat. sg.* **him** 63, 65, 67, 108, 118; *nom. pl.* **hi** 46, (RC **hiæ** 14, 16), **hie** 32, 48, etc.; *gen. pl.* **heora** 31, 155, **hira** 47; *dat. pl.* **him** 31, 83, 86, 88, 133.

heafod *n.* head; *dat. sg.* **heafdum** 63.

heah *adj.* high, lofty; *m. acc. sg.* **heanne** 40.

Heahfæder *m.* God the Father; *dat. sg.* **Heahfædere** 134.

healf *f.* half, side; *acc. sg.* **healfe** 20

heard *adj.* hard, severe; *sup. n. nom. sg.* **heardost** 87.

hebban *sv.* 6 to lift up, bear aloft 31.

hefig *adj.* oppressive, grim; *wk. n. dat. sg.* **hefian** 61.

help *f.* help, aid; *dat. sg.* **helpe** 102.

heofon *m.* heaven, sky; *gen. sg.* **heofenes** 64, (RC **heafunæs** 6, 16); *acc. pl.* **heofenas** 103; *gen. pl.* **heofona** 45; *dat. pl.* **heofenum** 85, 134, **heofonum** 140, 154.

heofonlic *adj.* heavenly; *m. acc. sg.* **heofonlicne** 148.

heofonrice *n.* kingdom of heaven; *gen. sg.* **heofonrices** 91.

heonon *adv.* hence, from here 132.

her *adv.* here 108, 137, 145.

hider *adv.* (to) here 103.

hilderinc *m.* warrior; *nom. pl.* **hilderincas** 61; *gen. pl.* **hilderinca** 72.

Hlaford *m.* Lord; *acc. sg.* 45, (RC **Hlafard** 6).

hleoðrian *wv.* 2 to speak; *3 sg. pret.*
  hleoðrode 26.

hlifian *wv.* 2 to rise, tower; *1 sg.*
  pres. **hlifige** 85.

hnigan *sg.* 1 to bend, bow down;
  1 sg. pret. **hnag** 59.

holmwudu *m.* wood on the hill;
  acc. sg. 91.

holt *m.n.* forest, wood; *gen. sg.*
  holtes 29.

hræw *m. n.* corpse; *nom. sg.* 72;
  acc. sg. 53.

hreotan *sv.* 2 to weep; *pp.*
  m. nom. pl. **hreotende** 70.

hreowcearig *adj.* sorrowful,
  troubled; *m. nom. n. acc. sg.* 25.

huru *adv.* certainly, indeed, how-
  ever 10.

hwa *pron.* who; *n. acc. sg.* **hwæt** 2,
  116.

hwænne *conj.* (the time) when 136.

hwær *conj.* where 112.

hwæt *interj.* what, well, lo, behold
  1, 90.

hwæð(e)re *conj.* however, but,
  nevertheless, yet 18, 24, 38, 42,
  57, 59, etc., (RC **hweþræ** 10).

hwil *f.* while, time; *acc. sg.* **hwile**
  24, 64, 70, 84, (RC **hwilæ** 16);
  dat. pl. as adv. **hwilum** at times
  22, 23.

hyht *m.* joy, hope; *nom. sg.* 126,
  hiht 148.

hyldan *wv.* 1 to bend, bow down
  45, (RC **hælda** 10).

ic *pron.* I; *nom. sg.* 1, 4, 13, etc.;
  acc. sg. **me** 30, 31, 32, etc.; *dat.*
  sg. 2, 4, 46, etc.; *nom. pl.* **we** 70;
  acc. pl. **us** 73, 75, 147a; *dat. pl.*
  147b; *dual acc.* **unc** 48, (RC
  ungket 7).

in *prep. w. dat* in 118.

inwidhlemm *m.* malicious wound;
  nom. pl. **inwidhlemmas** 47.

iu *adv.* long ago 28, 87.

k For RC forms with initial **k**,
  see corresponding head-words
  with initial **c**.

lædan *wv.* 1 to be raised, lifted up
  5.

læne *adj.* transitory, fleeting; *n.*
  dat. sg. **lænum** 109; *wk. n. dat.*
  sg. **lænan** 138.

lang *adj.* long; *f. acc. sg.* **lange** 24.

langunghwil *f.* time of longing;
  gen. pl. **langunghwila** 126.

lað *adj.* hostile, hateful; *sup. m.*
  nom. sg. **laðost** 88.

leode *f.* people, men; *dat. pl.*
  leodum 88.

leof *adj.* dear; *wk. m. voc. sg.* **leofa**
  78, 95.

leoht *n.* light; *dat. sg.* **leohte** 5.

libban *wv.* 3 to live; *3 pl. pres.*
  lifiaþ 134.

lic *n.* body; *gen. sg.* **lices** 63, (RC
  licæs 15).

licgan *sv.* 5 to lie; *pp. m.*
  nom. sg. **licgende** 24.

lif *n.* life; *acc. sg.* 147; *gen. sg.*
  lifes 8, 126; *dat. sg.* **life** 109,
  138.

limwerig *adj.* weary in limb; *m.*
  acc. sg. **limwerigne** 63, (RC **lim-**
  wœrignæ 14).

lof *m.* praise; *dat. sg.* **lofe** (BCI).

lyft *m. f. n.* air; *acc. sg.* (**on**) **lyft**
  on high 5.

lysan *wv.* 1 to redeem 41.

mænigo *f.* multitude; *dat. sg.*
  mænige 112, **manigeo** 151.

mære *adj.* great, glorious; *wk. f.*
  nom. sg. 12, 82; *wk. m. dat. sg.*
  mæran 69.

mæte *adj.* small; *n. dat. sg.* 69,
  124.

magan *pret. pres. v.* to be able; *1*
  sg. pres. **mæg** 85; *2 sg. pres.*
  miht 78; *3 sg. pres.* **mæg** 110;
  1 sg. pret. **meahte** 18, **mihte** 37.

man *m.* man, one, they, people;
  nom. sg. 73, 75, 112; *nom. pl.*
  menn 12 , 82, 128, (RC 7); *acc. pl.*
  (RC **men** 3), **menn** 93; *dat. pl.* **man-**
  num 96, 102.

mancyn(n) *n.* mankind, men;
  acc. sg. 41, 104; *gen. sg.* **man-**
  cynnes 33, 99.

manig *adj.* many; *m. gen. pl. as pron.* **manigra** 41; *f. dat. pl.* **manegum** 99; *m. dat. pl.* **manigeo** 151.

Maria *prop. name* Mary; *acc. sg.* **Marian** 92.

meðe *adj.* tired, exhausted; *m. nom. sg.* 65; *m. nom. pl.* sorrowful 69.

micel *adj.* great; *m. nom. sg.* **mycel** 130; *f. nom. sg.* 139; *m. dat. sg.* **mycle** 34, 60, 123; *wk. f. dat. sg.* **miclan** 102; *wk. n. dat. sg.* 65.

mid *prep. w. dat.* with, by among 7, 14, 16, 20, etc., (RC **miþ** 7, 12, 13); *as adv.* together with 106.

mid *adj.* middle; *f. dat. sg.* **midre** 2.

middangeard *m.* world; *acc. sg.* 104.

miht *f.* might, power; *dat. sg.* **mihte** 102.

mihtig *adj.* mighty, powerful; *m. nom. sg.* 151.

min *poss. adj.* my; *f. nom. sg.* 130, (BCI); *m. voc. sg.* 78, 95; *m. dat. sg.* **minum** 30.

mod *n.* heart, spirit; *dat. sg.* **mode** 122, 130.

modig *adj.* brave, courageous; *m. nom. sg.* 41.

modor *f.* mother; *acc. sg.* 92.

modsefa *m.* mind, spirit; *nom. sg.* 124.

moldærn *n.* grave, tomb; *acc. sg.* 65.

molde *f.* earth; *acc. sg.* **moldan** 12, 82.

motan *pret. pres. v.* to be able, may; *1 sg. pres.* **mot** 142; *1 sg. pres. subj.* **mote** 127.

mundbyrd *f.* allegiance, protection; *nom. sg.* 130.

nægl *m.* nail; *dat. pl.* **næglum** 46.

nah see **agan**.

nama *m.* name; *nom. sg.* (BCI); *dat. sg.* **nanam** 113.

ne *neg. particle* not 10, 35, 42, etc., (RC **ni** 4).

niht *f.* night; *dat. sg.* **nihte** 2.

nu *adv.* now 78, 80, 84, etc.

of *prep. w. dat.* of, from, out of 30, 49, 61, 66, etc.

ofer *prep. w. acc.* over, upon, throughout, more than, contrary to, against 12, 35, 82, 91, 94.

oft *adv.* often; *comp.* **oftor** 128.

on *prep.* in, on, upon, onto, into, at; *w. acc.* 5, 20, 32b, 40, etc.; *w. dat.* 9, 29, 32a, 41, 46, 50, 56, etc.; *postpositionally* 34, 98.

onbyrigan *wv.* 1 (*w. gen.*) to taste 114.

ond *conj.* and 12, 13, 22, etc., (RC 16).

onginnan *sv.* 3 to begin; *3 sg. pret.* **ongan** 19, 27, 73; *3 pl. pret.* **ongunnon** 65, 67; *3 pl. pres. subj.* **onginnen** 116.

ongyrwan *wv.* 1 to strip, disrobe; *3 sg. pret.* **ongyrede** 39, (RC **ondgeredæ** 1).

ongytan *sv.* 5 to perceive 18.

onlysan *wv.* 1 to redeem; *3 sg. pret.* **onlysde** 147.

onsendan *wv.* 1 to send forth, give up; *pp.* **onsended** 49.

onwreon *sv.* 1 to reveal, disclose; *2 sg. imper.* **onwreoh** 97.

open *adj.* open; *m. nom. pl.* **opene** 47.

oððæt *conj.* until 26, 32.

oððe *conj.* or, and 36.

reordberend *m.* speech-, voice-bearer, man; *nom. pl.* 3; *dat. pl.* **reordberendum** 89.

rest *f.* resting-place; *dat. sg.* **reste** 3.

restan *wv.* 1 to rest; *3 sg. pret.* **reste** 64, 69, (RC **restæ** 16).

rice *n.* kingdom; *acc. sg.* 119, 152.

rice *adj.* rich, powerful; *m. acc. sg.* **ricne** 44, (BCI), (RC **riicnæ** 5); *gen. pl.* **ricra** 131.

riht *adj.* right, proper, true; *m. acc. sg.* **rihtne** 89.

rod *f.* cross; *nom. sg.* 44, 136, (BCI); *acc. sg.* **rode** 119; *dat. sg.* **rode** 56, 131, (RC **rodi** 9).

sæl *m. f.* time. *nom. sg.* 80.

sar *adj.* sore, painful; *f. gen. pl.*
  sarra 80.

sare *adv.* sorely, deeply 59,
  (RC **saræ** 12).

sawl *f.* soul; *nom. sg.* 120; *dat. sg.*
  saule (BCl).

sceadu *f.* shadow, darkness; *nom.*
  sg. 54.

sceat *m.* corner, surface; *acc. pl.*
  sceatas 37; *dat. pl.* **sceatum** 8,
  43.

sceawian *wv.* 2 to see, behold;
  1 sg. pret. **sceawode** 137.

sceððan *sv.* 6 to harm, injure 47.

scima *m.* radance, light; *acc. sg.*
  sciman 54.

scinan *sv.* 1 to shine 15.

scir *adj.* clear, bright; *m. acc. sg.*
  scirne 54.

sculan *pret. pres. v.* to have to, be
  obliged to; *3 sg. pres.* **sceal** 119;
  1 sg. pret. **sceolde** 43, (RC
  scealde 4).

se, seo, þæt *def. art. demonst. adj.*
  and pron. the, that, those, who;
  m. nom. sg. 13, 42, 95, etc., *with*
  long vowel in pronominal func-
  tions 98, 107, 113, 145; *f. nom.*
  sg. **seo** 121; *n. nom. sg.* **þæt** 6,
  28a, 39, 74; *m. acc. sg.* **þone** 127;
  f. acc. sg. **þa** 20, 68, 119; *n. acc.*
  sg. **þæt** 18, 21, 28b, 58, 66; *m.*
  gen. sg. **þæs** 49, (RC 8); *m. n. dat. sg.*
  þam 9, 50, 58, etc., (RC 12),
  þan 122; *f. dat. sg.* **þære** 21,
  112, 131; *m. n. nom. pl.*
  þa 46, 61; *m. gen. pl.* **þara**
  86; *m. dat. pl.* **þam** 59, 143, 149,
  154.

seaþ *m.* pit; *dat. sg.* **seaþe** 75.

secan *wv.* 1 to seek out, visit 104,
  127; *3 pl. pret.* **sohton** 133.

secg *m.* man; *dat. pl.* **secgum** 59,
  (RC 12).

secgan *wv.* 3 to say, tell 1; *2 sg.*
  pres. subj. **secge** 96.

selest see **god**.

sendan *wv.* 1 to send, send forth
  (RC **senda** 8).

seolfor *n.* silver; *dat. sg.* **seolfre**
  77.

side *f.* side; *dat. sg.* **sidan** 49,
  (RC **sida** 8).

side *adv.* widely; **wide ond side**
  far and wide 81.

sigebeam *m.* wood of victory;
  nom. sg. 13; *acc. sg.* 127.

sigor *m.* victroy; *gen. pl.* **sigora** 67.

sigorfæst *adj.* triumphant, victori-
  ous; *m. nom. sg.* 150.

sinc *n.* treasure; *dat. sg.* **since** 23.

singal *adj.* continual, everlasting;
  f. nom. sg. 141.

siðfæt *m.* expedition, journey;
  dat. sg. **siðfate** 150.

siðian *wv.* 2 to go, journey, depart
  68.

siþþan *adv.* afterwards (RC 8).

sorg *f.* sorrow, distress; *gen. pl.*
  sorga 80; *dat. pl.* **sorgum** 20,
  59.

sorhleoð *n.* lament, dirge; *acc. sg.*
  67.

spedig *adj.* successful; *m. nom. sg.*
  151.

sprecan *sv.* 5 to speak 27.

stan *m.* stone; *dat. sg.* **stane** 66.

standan *sv.* 6 to stand 43, 62,
  (RC **standa** 8); *1 sg. pret.*
  stod 38; *1 pl. pret.*
  stodon 71; *3 pl. pret.* 7.

staðol *m.* position, foundation;
  dat. sg. **staðole** 71.

steam *m.* moisture; *dat. sg.*
  steame 62.

stefn *m.* trunk, root; *dat. sg.*
  stefne 30.

stefn *f.* voice, cry; *nom. sg.* 71.

stiðmod *adj.* resolute, courageous;
  m. nom. sg. 40.

stræl *m. f.* arrow, dart; *dat. pl.*
  strælum 62, (RC **strelum** 13).

strang *adj.* strong, firm, powerful;
  m. nom. sg. 40; *m. nom. pl.*
  strange 30.

sunu *m.* son; *nom. sg.* 150.

swa *conj.* as, even as, just as 92,
  108, 114; see **swylce (swa)**.

swætan *wv.* 1 to bleed 20.

swat *m. n.* blood; *gen. sg.* **swates**
  23.

swefn *n.* dream, vision; *gen. pl.*
swefna 1.

swiðra *comp. adj.* right (hand);
wk. f. acc. sg. **swiðran** 20.

swylce *conj.* and also 8, **swylce**
(swa) just as 92.

sylf *pron.* (him-, her-)self; *f. acc.*
sg. **sylfe** 92; *wk. m. nom. sg.*
sylfa 105.

syllic *adj.* unusual, wonderful,
marvellous; *m. nom. g.* 13;
comp. n. acc. sg. **syllicre** 4.

sym(b)el *n.* banquet, feast; *dat. sg.*
symle 141.

synn *f.* sin; *dat. pl.* **synnum** 13, 99,
146.

syþþan *adv.* afterwards 142.

syðþan *conj.* when, after 3, **siððan**
49, 71.

til *prep. w. dat.* to (RC 11, 12).

to *prep. w. dat.* to, into, at, for, of
2, 31, 42, 43, 58, etc.

treow *n.* tree, wood; *acc. sg.* 4, 14,
17, 25.

þa *adv.* then 27, 33, 35, 39, etc.

þa *conj.* when 36, 41, 42, 68,
151, 155, (RC 2).

þær *adv.* there, then 8, 9, 11, 24, 31,
etc., (RC **þer** 10, 16).

þær *conj.* where 139, 140, 141, 142,
156, when 123.

ðæron *adv.* therein 67.

þæt *conj.* that, so that, in that,
when 4, 19, 26, 29, etc., when that
34, 107.

þe *indecl. particle and rel. pron.*
who, which, that 111, 118,
137; **se þe** who, he who; *m.*
nom. sg. 98, 113, 145; *f. nom. sg.*
seo þe 121; *m. gen. pl.* **þara þe**
86; *m. dat. pl.* **þam þe** 149, 154.

þearle *adv.* severely, violently 52.

þegn *m.* thane, servant, follower;
nom. pl. **þegnas** 75.

þencan *wv.* 1 to think, consider,
intend; *3 sg. pres.* **þenceð** 121;
3 pl. pres. **þencaþ** 115.

þenian *wv.* 1 to stretch out 52.

þeoden *m.* prince, lord; *dat. sg.*

þeodne 69.

þes, þeos, þys *demonst. adj. and*
pron. this; *f. nom. sg.* **þeos** 12,
82; *m. acc. sg.* **þysne** 104; *f. acc.*
sg. **þas** 96, (BCI); *n. dat. sg.* **þyssum**
83,109, **þysson** 138.

þolian *wv.* 2 to endure, suffer;
3 pl. pret. **þolodan** 149.

þonne *adv.* then 107, 115, 117, 139,
142.

þonne *conj.* than 128.

þrowian *wv.* 2 suffer; *3 sg. pret.*
þrowode 84, 98, 145.

þyrmfæst *adj.* glorious; *m. nom.*
sg. 84.

ðu *pron.* thou; *nom. sg.* 78, 96;
acc. sg. **þe** 95.

þurfan *pret. pres. v.* to need; *3 sg.*
pres. **þearf** 117.

þurh *prep. w. acc.* through, by
virtue of, by reason of 10, 18,
119.

þurhdrifan *sv.* 1 to drive through,
pierce; *3 pl. pret.* **þurhdrifan** 46.

þyncan *wv.* 1 (*impers. w. dat.*) to
seem, appear; *3 sg. pret.* **þuhte**
4.

þystro *f.* darkness, gloom; *nom. pl.*
52.

unc unket see **ic**.

under *prep. w. dat.* under, beneath
55, 85.

unforht *adj. m. nom. sg.* unafraid
110; very afraid, terrified 117.

up *adv.* up 71.

uppe *adv.* up, above 9.

wæd *f.* dress, clothing; *dat pl.*
wædum 15, 22.

wæfersyn *f.* show, spectacle; *dat.*
sg. **wæfersyne** 31.

wæta *m.* wetness, moisture; *dat.*
sg. **wætan** 22.

wann *adj.* dark, black; *f. nom. sg.*
55.

we see **ic**.

weald *m.* forest; *gen. sg.* **wealdes**
17.

Wealdend *m.* Ruler, Lord; *nom. sg.*
111, 155; *acc. sg.* 67; *gen. sg.*

Wealdendes 17, 53; *dat. sg.*
Wealdende 121.

Weard *m.* Guardian, Lord; *nom. sg.*
91.

weg *m.* way, path; *acc. sg.* 88.

well *adv.* well, fully 129, 143.

wenan *wv.* 1 to hope, look for;
1 sg. pres. **wene** 135.

wendan *wv.* 1 to alter, change 22.

weorc *n.* work, pain; *nom. acc. sg.* 79.

weorod *n.* host, multitude; *dat.*
sg. **weorode** 69, 152, **werede** 124;
gen. pl. **weruda** 51.

weorþian *wv.* 2 to honour, adore
129; *3 pl. pres.* **weorðiað** 81.

weorðlice *adv.* worthily, magnifi-
cently 17.

wepan *sv.* 7 to weep; *3 sg. pret.*
weop 55.

werg *m.* outlaw, criminal; *acc. pl.*
wergas 31.

wesan *anom. v.* to be 110, 117; *3 sg.*
pres. **is** 80, 97, 126, etc., **bið** 86; *3*
pl. pres. **syndon** 46; *1 sg. pret.*
wæs 20, 21, 29, etc.; *2 sg. pret.*
wæs 6, 10, 13, etc.; *3 pl. pret.*
wæron 8; *3 sg. pres. subj.* **si(e)**
112, 144.

wide *adv.* widely, **wide ond side**
far and wide 81.

wif *n.* woman; *gen. pl.* **wifa** 94.

willa *m.* desire, purpose; *nom. sg.*
129.

willan *anom. v.* to will, wish,
intend; *1 sg. pres.* **wylle** 1;
3 sg. pres. **wile** 107; *3 sg. pret.*
wolde 34, 41; *3 pl. pret.* **woldon**
68; *3 sg. pret. subj.* **wolde** 113.

wite *n.* punishment, torture; *dat.*
sg. 61; *gen. pl.* **wita** 87.

wolcen *m. n.* cloud, sky; *dat. pl.*
wolcnum 53, 55.

wom *m. n.* sin, stain; *dat. pl.*
wommum 14.

word *n.* word, command; *acc. sg.*
35; *dat. sg.* **worde** 111; *acc. pl.*
word 27; *dat. pl.* **wordum** 97.

woruld *f.* world; *gen. sg.* **worulde**
133.

wrað *adj.* cruel; *f. gen. pl.* **wraðra**
51.

wudu *m.* (piece of) wood; *nom. sg.*
27.

wuldor *n.* glory, splendour; *gen.*
sg. **wuldres** 14, 90, 97, 133; *dat.*
sg. **wuldre** 135, 143, 155.

wunian *wv.* 2 to live, dwell, be
121, 143; *3 pl. pres.* **wuniaþ**
135; *3 pl. pret.* **wunedon** 3, 155.

wynn *f.* joy; *dat. pl. as adv.*
pleasantly, beautifully **wyn-**
num 15.

wyrcan *wv.* 1 to make 65 (BCI
wyrican).

wyrd *f.* fate, event; *nom. sg.* 74;
gen. pl. **wyrda** 51.

ymbclyppan *wv.* 1 to clasp,
embrace; *3 sg. pret.* **ymbclypte**
42.